Futures

2018 Poetry Collection

Futures represents our student authors as accurately as possible.
Every effort has been made to print each poem
as it was submitted with minimal editing
of spelling, grammar, and punctuation.
All submissions have been formatted to this compilation.

Published by
The America Library of Poetry
P.O. Box 978
Houlton, ME 04730
Website: www.libraryofpoetry.com
Email: generalinquiries@libraryofpoetry.com

Printed in the United States of America.

THE AMERICA
LIBRARY OF POETRY

ISBN: 978-0-9966841-4-9

Contents

Poetry by Division

Futures

Foreword

There are two kinds of writers in the world.
There are those who write from experience,
and those who write from imagination.
The experienced, offer words that are a reflection of their lives.
The triumphs they have enjoyed, the heartaches they have endured;
all the things that have made them who they are,
they graciously share with us, as a way of sharing themselves,
and in doing so, give us, as readers, someone to whom we may relate,
as well as fresh new perspectives
on what may be our common circumstances in life.
From the imaginative,
come all the wonderful things we have yet to experience;
from sights unseen, to sounds unheard.
They encourage us to explore the limitless possibilities
of our dreams and fantasies,
and aid us in escaping, if only temporarily,
the confines of reality and the rules of society.
To each, we owe a debt of gratitude;
and rightfully so, as each provides a service of equal importance.
Yet, without the other, neither can be truly beneficial.
For instance, one may succeed in accumulating a lifetime of experience,
only to consider it all to have been predictable and unfulfilling,
if denied the chance to chase a dream or two along the way.
Just as those whose imaginations run away with them never to return,
may find that without solid footing in the real world,
life in fantasyland is empty.
As you now embark, dear reader,
upon your journey through these words to remember,
you are about to be treated to both heartfelt tales of experience,
and captivating adventures of imagination.
It is our pleasure to present them for your enjoyment.
To our many authors,
who so proudly represent the two kinds of writers in the world,
we dedicate this book, and offer our sincere thanks;
for now, possibly more than ever,
the world needs you both.

Paul Wilson Charles
Editor

Editor's Choice Award

The Editor's Choice Award is presented
to an author who demonstrates not only
the solid fundamentals of creative writing,
but also the ability to elicit an emotional response
or provide a thought provoking body of work
in a manner which is both clear and concise.

You will find "I Won't Forget"
by Laura Ospina on page 161 of Futures

2018
Spirit of Education
For Outstanding Participation

Ernest Becker Middle School

Las Vegas, Nevada

Presented to participating students and faculty
in recognition of your commitment
to literary excellence.

Division I

Grades
3-5

Freedom
by Matthew Taylor

When in despair,
The lock is the key to freedom.

Language
by Saige Higgins

Language to speak
Language to communicate
English, Spanish, and French
Language.

Midnight
by Jazmen Silvey

Black sky
Very scary
Kids roaming the long street
They saw something in the bushes
They screamed

Shooting Star
by Julia Pilla

Shooting star, shooting star
You shine like a gold bar.
I see you at night
Tucked in bed while you shine your light.

Meg, Peg and Larry
by Ashlynn Higgins

There once was a girl named Peg
Who walked on a wooden leg
She had a bunny named Larry
Larry wasn't very hairy
She loved to play with Meg

Diamonds
by Benicio Vallejo

Diamonds, diamonds how they glow.
How they are made, I want to know!
Are they blue are they green, I wonder if I have to pay a lien!
Maybe I can find them, if I go mine them!
If I use the right tool, I will find this beautiful jewel!

July
by Hector Rivas

In July birds go.
Just like when moon comes tonight.
But sometimes it goes.

The Girl of My Dreams
by Charles Decunto

I liked the girl of my dreams.
But she left me when she got in her teens.
Now I hate the girl of my dreams.

Flowers
by Shiley Johnson

Flowers are like people
Different -
Sizes
Colors
Shapes
Personalities

The Ocean
by Katherine D'Arienzo

Dance with the waves,
Move with the sea,
Let the rhythm of the waves
Set your soul free.

Softball
by Sarah Voss

Bats, gloves, players
Coaches, balls, umpires, field
Parents cheering to hit that ball.
Play it!

Pencil
by Eva Wymer

Go inside a pencil, are there drawings and stories waiting to be spilled out.
Waiting to be sharpened, waiting to bring art, positivity, peace or destruction.
As the lead hits the page to create. Does a pencil have a mind of its own,
Or a city filled with artists waiting to create something NEW.

My Food
by Caleb Serrer

I always like my mom's food.
If I didn't, that would be rude.

Bitter
by Lilly Glaubach

It was cold as the arctic outside
Frigid, freezing, and bitter
Even if you put on enough jackets and coats
You still would be colder than ice.
But every Christmas Eve
You hear a jolly "Ho-Ho-Ho" from up above
It's Santa speaking to the world
But even his voice is cold and bitter
The icy night was a day in a blizzard
Cold, bitter, and polar.

Water Show
by Laila Toribio

Shades of black, white, and grey,
Appear with a salty splash.
Sing a song, loud and clear,
As a blow of cool water splashes down,
One splash for each acrobatic trick.
Watchful eyes from a crowd above,
Cheering for the serene sighting.
Like raindrops in a cloud,
The boats float over to visit,
To see the enormous music maker,
Whisper a melodic song.

Flying
by Wally Crosby

She just flew as high as the sky goes,
She flew like a fly, like a bird, like a plane,
And you won't come back down,
But I need you to come, come back down,
So that I can keep you company,
Instead of the sky and space between us,
Of course you won't listen to me
Because you don't care for me anyway.
That's all for me,
So farewell for you and me.
Now listen to what she wants to say about me.

My Dad
by Sahana Gummadi

I have a dad
He's never sad
He's always glad
And sometimes he's rad.

Life At Home
by Kimberly Mensch

I love my home.
It's been there since I was born.
I was raised in that home.
It brings memories back.
I miss the memories so much.
I give Mom and Dad lots of hugs.
Every morning when I wake up ...
I remember that I love my family
and my life.
This was our loving home

A Trip To Disneyland
by Hannah Zimmerman

On the way to Disneyland,
I heard music, la ... la ... la ...
I heard the train, choo, choo,
It was awesome except ...
The sun was hot, but I wish it was not.
Boom, Zoom, Zoom ...
the roller coasters take off!
I saw pretty princesses and blue bears.
I saw a brook, and to the water I took.
I love Disneyland and I hope you do too!

The Forest
by Carsen McKay

The forest is green and ready for you
to listen to the birds that can give you a clue.
The forest can be there or here as long as it's ready
for you to say the forest is good
if you want to be with the trees, as long as the trees like you.
The forest is in you and me
but to believe the forest must believe in you.
If you need trees the forest is there and sometimes not
sometimes you need to look
- when you look and find a forest, make it your friend.

Fourth of July
by Gabe Squires

Tastes like watermelon.
Smells like fresh shooting stars.
Looks like colors flashing across the night sky.
Sounds like booming fireworks.
Feels like a hot oven.

Quinten
by Quinten Coppedge

Quinten
Nerdy, funny, bookish, creative
Brother of Christian
Lover of games, Star Wars and dogs
Who fears rodents, heights, and failing a test
Who would like to see the National Aerospace Museum,
Redwood National Park and Norway
Resident of Montana
Coppedge

Colors
by Emily Nelson

Red, blue, purple, and green
Alligators look so mean
Orange, yellow, brown, and black
I put my lunch in a paper sack
Teal, gray, gold, and white
Don't worry my dog doesn't bite
Silver, mint, and indigo too
I wait for the bus with Sue
So many colors to use
I just don't know what to choose

Siblings
by Harley Dobry

One's name is Anna, she won't eat her banana
One's name is Crystal, she is very blissful
One's name is Sean, he thinks he's big and strong
One's name is Steven, he's nice, fair, and even
One's name is Squishy, he loves his toy fishy
One's name is Angel (no she's not from Heaven), she's as old as 10 plus 7
One's name is Sky, don't ask me why
One's name is Trent, our dad's name is Brent
Then there's Mom, who is the bomb!
My name is Harley, this poem has come to an end, so I am sorry

The Joys of Life
by Madison deVaux

When life may seem unfair
Look closer and you'll see something else.
You'll see the group of friends you always hung out with.
You'll see the family that always cared for you.
And when times may be strict, that means they just love you more.
Yes, life may be full of stress and strife
But if you look a little closer, you'll see the joys of life.

The Beach
by Ethan Buys

The beach has a soft breeze with a
Harmless sun setting in the horizon.
You can feel the sand covering your
Feet and hands while you smell the ocean.
You can see kid's enjoyment with water and splashing each other.
You can hear the waves washing
Up on the shore.
You think about your life and know that you're on the right track.
Thinking ... sleepy ... and good ...

I See ...
by Cayla Morgan

I see someone who is insecure about how they look.
I see someone who is not good enough.
"I can't walk into school like this!"
I say, for, I know real school isn't like how it is in a book.
I need to cover myself with makeup, hoping someone will notice.
Then I give myself down talk, saying I still don't look pretty.
Saying I need to be more like the kids that curse, but I make a new verse.
I see potential, I see confidence
I see that I can be good enough.

Bruce the Goose
by Haley Gordon

There was a goose, whose name was Bruce. In games he never liked to lose.
Then one day, Bruce went to play a game of ostrich-egg kick.
His team tried hard but lagged behind and Bruce was feeling sick.
Bruce gave up hope and sobbed, "This is the end for us.
All that's left to do, is tie my shoe." He bent over on the grass.
While he was busy crying, the ostrich egg came near.
Bruce straightened his knee to kick away a bee and heard a distant cheer.
Then Bruce became a hero. He was elected most valuable goose.
He'd accidently scored the winning goal and didn't have to lose.

Gun
by Cole Clardy

Gun
Loud, flame
Distance, hot, big
Small, fast, sharp, long
Cold, smooth, shiny
Quiet, pointed
Sword

The Frog and the Log
by Cheyenne Stein

There was a frog
On a log
Jumping from log to log
Who likes to snug
Who eats slugs
Then came a pug
Who likes to play
And likes to stay
But he had to pay

Hold On
by Shawn Mack

Hold on
Hold on to friends
Even if they aren't the best
Hold on to Montana
Even if it is tough
Hold on to your family
Even if times are hard
Hold on to good things
Even if you are sad

Dad
by Kiahna Hirmann

Dad is my safety
Dad is there
Dad is my heart, my soul
Dad is the one who made me his
Dad I love
Dad is the good-night "sis bear"
Dad is my world
Dad is the color in my blood
Dad is the one!

My Best Friend
by Keeley Kirkegard

You're my best friend
You've been with me through every bend
Struggle and strife
All my life
That is why
It's always been you and I
You and me together
Best friends forever

She Forgets
by Anthony Busa

She forgets she's present
She forgets she's near
Maybe she forgets life
Or maybe how to hear
She forgets to laugh
She forgets to cheer
Time is a bandit
Time is a thief, it robs you of your memory
She forgets that too.

One Stormy Day
by Ahmiyah Evans

One day it was storming
and Milly and Jake wanted to go outside and play.
They got their boots and coats on and went.
They found a bunny stuck in the mud.
They helped her out and took her inside.
The next day they woke up and the bunny had escaped.
So much panic, then we found her by the door.
So happy!

Depression
by Vania Mendez

You might ask, "Why are you sad?"
I would always tell you, "I'm fine."
But what you really want to know is,
"Why are there cuts in your wrist?"
I might say, "It was the cat."
But what is really going on is
I'm stuck in this dark and sad place called depression.
And the only one that can save me from this misery is you.
But from now on, I will remain in this sad and dark place.

Friends
by Lilly Hilliker

Cool, funny and smart
always have your back
That's what friends are for
When you're sad
There is always someone
To cheer you up
When you have a bad day
There is always someone
To make it better
When you have a problem
There is always someone
To help you out
When you need a hug
There is always someone
Behind you with open arms
Cool, funny and smart
My friends have my back
And I have theirs

Why Is?
by Gracelynn Wood

Why are there flowers?
Why are there books?
Why is there wrestling?
Why is America, America?
Why are there 50 states?
Why are there 12 months in a year?
Why is it that babies have to stay in the womb for 9 months?
Why are there bugs?
Why are there bunnies?
Who made shoes?
Why are there dogs?
Why are there cats?
Why are there feet?
Why is there love?
Why is there paper?
Why are there hands?
Why is there money?
Why is there food?
Why are there toys?
Why is there a sky?
Why is there school?
Why are there ducks?
Why are there letters?
Why are there babies?

Belle
by Heidirae Malin

Belle is beautiful
Belle is bright
Belle is also one-of-a-kind
Belle looks like a cow
Although she doesn't go bow-wow
Belle is my sun
She also like hot dog buns
She does the "Wild Run"
She is lots of fun
She likes human food
And sometimes has a mood
I love Belle with all my heart
This may seem funny but she sometimes farts
You may think, "Dude, she's just a dog"
And she eats like a hog
But I love Belle with all my heart
And nothing can stop that
Not even you
And I know that's true

America!!!
by Hampton Newman

Blessed is America, blessed of all kind
Blessed are the loyal, for they are great and kind
Blessed is America, blessed is our flag,
Blessed are the people, with high responsibility,
That love America and her flag
America runs free, blessed is America, freedom everywhere,
Blessed is its name, it's fearless and fair,
Her flag waves for freedom, and America's still the same
Free for all justice with love, joy and fame
Blessed is America and all her history,
Blessed is her history and all it's done for me!
Blessed are the people who died for all of us,
We love them and we thank them, for all they have done for us.
Blessed is America and all the sandy shores,
And all the rising oceans and all the birds that soar
Blessed is America and all the green grass,
With water and soil, which makes it grow fast!
God has blessed America in an extraordinary way
And wants us to be happy in each and every way!

Thoughts ...
by Selah Brown

Thoughts ...
In your head
And
Out again.

Art
by Samantha Littlejohn

Colors filled the page
With soft colors and bright lights
She painted with sage
She grabbed her pastels and colored pencils
to add what she thought was right
She paused drawing to get an outlook,
But all she saw was a colorful background,
She grabbed her pen and outlined to change the look
This piece was alive and reached out with sound
"This needs more!" she exclaimed with a gleam in her eye
She grabbed her brushes and started to stroke
She saw a great big sky
She took a break and drank her Coke
She went back to her canvas,
and colored it with a wide variety of color
She, with her pencil and colors, she drew wonders
It looks like she has drawn the mountains of Kansas.

Planets
by Nathan Greer

Neptune is beautiful, with swirls of light and dark blue.
I like the colors that it chose.
It's a blue ball of gas.
Jupiter is exciting, with a nearly everlasting storm on it.
And when it fades out, if it ever does, a new one will develop soon after.
Such small dust rings, but with 63 moons, for a massive gas giant.
Saturn is fantastic, it's a giant gas ball.
Twelve moons all around,
And bright rings of ice both broad and wide.
Pluto is fascinating, like a stuck comet.
A big ice ball hurled at the Sun,
But never made it.
Uranus is interesting, and used to spin like the others.
But a meteorite hit it and now it spins on its side,
Unique and special.
Mars is amazing. It used to be another Earth,
But now it is the Red Planet. A dry and dusty desert.
It may have supported life long, long ago.

The Lovely Snow
by Madeline Beattie

The sun was a beautiful balloon rising in the sky.
Windy, cold, freezing.
The snowflake falling was music to my ears.
Falling down like mini pillows from the sun.
On and on and it never stops.
Snowy.

My Pigs
by Caylee McPherson

I love my pigs.
And so does my brother.
They don't look like twigs.
And definitely not my mother
Most pigs have great personalities.
They always bring me back to reality.
I hope to win a pig show.
And the pig will be named Joe.
Sometimes the judges are cross.
But I act like a boss.
I want to have a lovable pig.
And it can have a wig.
I hope to have baby pigs soon.
And they will be born at noon.
They can be messy.
But I love my piggies.

Penguins
by Gabriel Dubrinsky

Penguins like to waddle in the snow
They play and slide with happiness and pride
These animals can swim and glide through the water
The fishes stand no chance against these creatures
Though they cannot fly, this is not a lie
They "fly" on the ice and it is very nice
It looks like they don't have knees
They try to hide it but we can see
They have knees inside of them
Penguins and puffins are not the same
Puffins can fly but penguins can't
They may look like family
But they don't even know each other
The little blue penguin is the smallest
But the Emperor penguin is the tallest
And the Adélie penguin is the cutest

Dance With Your Heart
by Hannah Weller

The music starts
And your heart is bursting with emotion
The feeling starts with the core
And spreads throughout the entire body
To the fingers, to the toes
And you start to DANCE

My Trip To the Zoo
by Brooklyn Teel

My trip to the zoo was a hoot
I even heard the train nearby go toot
I saw a lion in a cage
and a monkey rampage
I heard an elephant go thump
and the camel had more than 1 hump
I saw a really big bear
and it gave me a slight scare
I saw an otter dive
then more people arrived
I saw some penguins cuddle
and hyenas huddle
Then we walked out the door
but I wanted to see more,
Well this talk has been fun
but I got to run.

Snow Day, Hooray!
by Brooklyn Bilbrey

I was at school one day
when I saw a snowflake fall,
then another and another,
by noon it was 5 feet tall!
I said, "SNOW DAY, HOORAY!"
the teacher said it too,
she was so happy she seemed to glow,
we had some celebrating to do.
She yelled, "YES!!!" at the top of her lungs
she whispered, "Oh dear. Oh my."
"Sorry kids, you must leave early."
which sounded like a lie.
So she sent us quickly out the door,
I saw her speeding by,
we had a new teacher the following day,
I'll always wonder why.

Leaves
by Cash Dicketts

Red, orange, yellow
These are some colors of leaves.
Leaves dance and play in the wind.
They float around without a care.
They touch the ground very softly.
They crunch and crackle under the feet of little children.

Until ...
by Samantha Rother

I wave goodbye this early morn',
My heart sharply torn
I hope to see you once again,
For now I shall hang my chin.
The sand beneath my feet,
Later, here I stand, we shall meet.
The soft breeze through my hair,
A lonely feeling we shall share.
I long for you day and night.
I try to stay hopeful with all my might.
The waves crash up and down,
Yet from me you hear no sound.
I yearn and cry for my love,
As I gaze upon the stars above.
I know that again we shall meet,
And it shall be tender and sweet.

Ice Cream
by Serenity Cressor

Ice cream, ice cream, cherry on top, sprinkle sprinkles on the top
Cherry, vanilla, banana, rocky road,
Mint chocolate chip, cookie dough, coconut, cheesecake, and custard too
1 scoop, 2 scoops, 3 scoops more, with a drizzle of caramel, chocolate,
or a squirt of whipped creammmm!
Ice cream is sweet as candy, sweeter than honey, creamy smooth ice cream!
Ice cream tastes like joy in my mouth.
Chocolate, cinnamon, waffle, plain cones too, they're all calling my name
Sweet sweet sweet ice cream, yummy yummy yummy ice cream
Better than honey.
Better than water, colder than ice cold water
Ice cream falling from the sky
Colorful colorful ice cream, ice cream is blue as the sky
I know when ice cream is good when it trickles down my chin,
Dripping down my hand, and never hitting the floor
The ice cream I like makes me want more more more

Predators
by Hamid Rahmatullah

Lion
Strong, clever,
Creeping, hunting, running,
Mane, claws, predators, scales, teeth,
Swimming, leaping, grabbing,
Scaly, scary,
Crocodile

Passion
by Hayley Herb

Passion
The joy of life, relieves my strife
A spark in my head, a light in my heart
Passion
Reach for the stars, a passion is ours
A story to write, it lights up the night
Passion
When things go wrong, motivation keeps me strong
Live in the moment, be positive, own it
Passion
Look up at the sky, your heart knows you try
A passion is pleasure when you're under the weather
Passion
The sky is the limit, go out and win it
Passion

I See Light
by Mackenzie Kanouff

One day I was flying a kite
I thought what if I never see light
Then I drank some Sprite
That night I saw something bright
Could it be my sight
That's so amazingly bright
It just might
To my parents it was a fright
To me it feels like I have a new height
So I drank some more Sprite, it made me see light
The next morning when I woke up
I saw the color of my pup
Then I went to go play with my friend, Mark
I told him about my spark
I stayed the night with Ted
Now I must go to bed.

One Night
by Ryan Matthiesen

As I look out at the night sky
I see a dozen fireflies
When I get all tucked in my bed
Although my home is in a shed
But then I hear the door creak
I really start to freak
I scream, "No, don't eat me crocodile,"
He replies, "I think your imagination is running wild."

The Dark Room
by Ashton Morrell

As you enter through the doorway
The curtains wave as it's saying goodbye
Your heartbeat, pounding
Like drums
Ears ring like bells
As you see the new room
Darkness teasing you
Waiting to be entered
Light above
Fidgeting with fear
Lurking like shadows
Creeping away
You step forward into the dark room
The light fading like echoes
The darkness swallows you whole

Track
by Owen Clark

I am warming up in my new cleats,
While listening with my sick beats.
I am about to start,
Which I am running against Paul Blart.
I am running one mile,
Which might take a while.
We just now started,
And I darted.
I stop halfway because I am tired,
And what do you know I just got past,
And now I am in last.
And yes he won,
By a ton.
Thank goodness he forgot his medal,
Now I know next time it is pedal to the metal.

Summertime
by Jaiden Mason

Bethlehem School is so cool.
But I would rather be home playing in the pool.
Hot summer days are on the way.
There is no way I could possibly stay.
So while I am out for summer break,
I am going to make all the memories I can make.
Yes, summer days are coming fast,
but summer days will go by so fast.
Then comes August, it's back to school.
to learn all I can, because I am no fool.

What Goes On In My Mind
by Danica Bliss

Once there was a toy that turned into a boy.
Then went to a zoo, he saw a pearl turn into a girl.
I guess you can say it was love at first sight.
Then a few years later, the toy that turned into a boy
and the pearl that turned into a girl got married
and moved to St. Mary and had two kids.
Then the brother Tarry was kind of scary
and he said he saw a fairy that went to Dalary
and had a lot of dairy, and got a bellyache
and died a few weeks later.
Then the boy woke up and the dead fairy and Scary-Tarry
and the pearl that turned into a girl
and the toy that turned into a boy,
All went back to Dreamland.

Wolf's Day
by Peyton Evans

There once was a wolf
He would always howl at the moon
He would howl and howl until sunrise
He'll hunt his food until dawn
He will enjoy his perfect feast
All the food will be gone
Then sleep for the rest of the day
Wake up at night to hear the wolves howl through the night
The different howls create a song
He listens to the music as he goes and starts to hunt
He hunts but doesn't find anything
The rest of the night is put to rest
Sleeping away through the night
The moon shines bright

My Friend Nature
by Brian Rosas-Rios

My friend Nature is bright.
It has apples that are sweet and ripe.
I like to play day and night.
I love to plant flowers and crops.
I try to keep my flowers big and tall.
I like to water trees big or small.
My world has to be clean.
I love my creatures red or blue.
Even if it has polka-dots and purple stripes,
My friend Nature has a surprise every time.

Our Good Old American Flag
by Lily Vickers

In 1776,
our flag was placed in Fort Stanwix.
Our flag stands for freedom, yes, that is true.
It has many colors, like Red, White, and Blue.
The white of the stripes tells us
that our intentions are purer than the water rain brings,
and our ideas are higher than oh, so many things.
The red reminds us of our courage and willingness to sacrifice,
for our friends, our family, and everyone else in our life.
The blue behind the stars, plain as can be,
shows that our country has vigilance and justice, as everyone can see.
Yes, our flags may be old, some are faded too,
but they stand proud against the sky so blue.
This, I know, is true.

A Dog In Heaven
by Jalin Basham

A dog is family, treat them right
Their smile always makes me bright.
They have their fun to play and run
I wish there was another one.
To make it up and save the day
And show them how to say "hooray."
Take the time to play it safe
Teach them how to make a break.
When the time is almost done
Always hope there's another one,
To show they are not forgotten
remember the love that was broughten.
Just know they are in a better plain,
and no longer feel that pain!

Little Joe
by Layney Robertson

Little Joe was a turtle
His best friend was named Mertle
They went to the lake
They met Jake the snake
Jake the snake ate Pat the rat
Pat the rat loves to chat
His best friend is a bat
They went to the lake
To play all day
In the shade

Montana, Montana
by Tristyn Euliss

Montana, Montana, how far will you be,
I wish I was there to be and to see,
All the great things you have,
To the wild horses,
Just running life's courses,
The buffalo so wild and free,
To the great mountain lion that stands before me,
Custer, who died at the Battle of Little Big Horn,
Where the great chiefs were born,
To see the wolf howl,
At the great hooting owl,
The great mountains standing so tall,
That hold it all,
Montana, Montana, created just for me

The Redwood Tree
by Caleb Longnecker

I was walking through the woods one day
And then I saw something in my way.
I cheered with glee
As I saw a redwood tree.
It has beautiful sap
It was a nice place to nap.
It was a sight to see
From the squirrels in the branches
To the bees doing dances.
Then I thought
If this tree fell down
I would have a serious frown.
When I grew up I bought the land
And owned the woods, a happy man.

Night
by Lakin Cash

The night is dark
The wind is cold
The moon is up
The sun is set
The stars are bright
The night is quiet
The wind is calm
The moon is full
The sun is down
The stars are twinkling
Night, night, night
The wind makes me shiver in the night.

Sheep and Wolves
by Dakota Whisenhunt

Sheep always run when they have fun,
They even do some funny puns.
They love to have a race,
They also like to play chase.
They chase people all the way to the pond,
And run around until they fall to the ground.
They never frown all the way to town.
Wolves are big and bad.
They love to brag even when they do,
They can't count to two.
Sometimes they get very blue.
When wolves find sheep they want to eat them,
Therefore they just can't greet them.

Nature's Wonders
by Praneel Patel

The wind blows the ocean waves rise
Birds call and lions roar
The same happens on the ocean floor
The fish squeak, the sharks peek for animals to eat
The bird catches a snake and it feels like a feat
In the wild cheetahs run
A lion catches a fox for fun
Hunters come for a chicken when it sleeps
But it wakes up with a peep
It runs away and thinks its escape is set
But hunters trap it in a net
Nature is great without a doubt
But loveliness is what it's all about!

Painting a Picture
by Emily Beter

Paintbrush swiftly slides right
Making trees that look so bright.
Mountains high and valleys low
Paintbrush making look aglow.
After I put in the trees
Clouds make way to calm the seas.
Water and oceans up the shore
Looking up make mountains more.
Grassy and politely keen
Valley sneaks below the scene.
Left some water right beside him
Then, comes last the ocean tides in.
Sun shines bright picture almost done
Leaves from trees complete the sun.
Blades of grass colored lightly green
Flowers scatter like jumping beans.
So finally, let's redeem
With prairies low and seas so deep
Last of all, picture's complete.

Swerving Emotions
by Kaitlin Simmons

Anger, sadness, fury, madness
Emotions break loose from me before I can stop
Emotions that rattle my head and control me
Condensing my thoughts, I am forced to speak
Emotion will call to me swiftly and repeatedly
Forcefully lulling me into his trap
Emotions rush through my confused head
Am I confused, happy, surprised, sad?
The genuine emotion is unknown and useless
Thoughts are flushed out of my head
They are replaced with strain and agony
Regret starts to fill my head and mind
Despicable thoughts seep through me and I can't think!
Soon pain sears through me as I struggle to say something
Pointless thoughts whirl in my head
I try to breathe, and stop my rant
My heartbeat steadies and is normal again
My emotion changes, a calm, assured, relaxed change
Emotions do change, but I'll stay strong!

The Little Puppy
by Shelby Lancaster

There once was a little dog.
It liked to sit on a log.
Its name was Bruse.
Bruse liked to get loose.
Bruse likes to play fetch.
Bruse also likes to play catch.
He dances around like a moose.
He likes to steal cups of juice.
He likes to ride in the car.
When he's in the car, he likes going far.
He likes my other dog.
He likes to play in the fog.
He's just a little puppy.
He's like a little guppy.
He likes to sit near logs.
He eats like a hog.
He likes to take naps.
He likes to wear wool hats.
I have a dog that likes to get loose.
That is my dog, Bruse.

Treasure
by Adaline Paton

There is a new treasure to seek.
I believe it's on Cloud Mountain's peak.
so I climb, and I climb, what do I find?
A toucan with a long purple beak.
The treasure may be buried in sand.
I believe it's on a tropical island.
so I row, and I row, what do I find?
A blue walrus you can hold in your hand.
The treasure may be down below,
In the blue ocean's shallows.
so I swim, and I swim, what do I find?
An octopus who stubbed his eighth toe.
It might be up in the sky.
Well, I hope I can fly ...
so I soar, and I soar, what do I find?
A dragon with one flaming red eye.
It's the treasure of nature and magic I see ...
Right there in front of me!
But then I wake in my room,
to my alarm clock's tune
And then realize it was all just a dream!

Safe Place
by Cendra Carter

Falling on my knees
Crying in my safe place
Where I read
It's calming.
I climb a tree
The wind flowing through my hair
The moon shining in the night sky
This is where I relax.

Tiger
by Jade Rogers

The tiger comes ...
On huge tiger paws ...
It pounces on its prey ...
But, instead of eating the prey ...
It just walks away ...
Leaving food for other animals ...
Right there,
On the soft mossy ground.

I Wish Spring Would Come
by Charlie-Jo Thompson

Oh, I wish spring would come
It's my favorite time of year
It has yet to show its happy face
The winter is still here
With no green grass, I am so sad
Flowers make me glad
Oh, I wish spring would come
It's my favorite time of year

Our Sky
by Alexa Zientara

Palest colors tint the wakening,
While black seeps away with its starry night.
Like an ocean tide slipping off
As pink and lavender spread the dawn's light.
The sun arises like an eager child
Tossing off covers from this newest day,
Making the sky brighten with hints of blue
that bloom the azure of a sun-sparkled bay

Predator and Prey
by Cherish Swedberg

Predator
vicious, cruel,
hunting, stalking, tracking,
sharks, lions, rabbits, zebras,
hiding, fearing, running,
innocent, fearful,
Prey

Don't Be Tardy
by Annabel Hicks

Don't be tardy
go to school
Don't be tardy
that's not cool!!
Don't be tardy
go to school
Don't be tardy
I am not a fool!!

Hiking On a Mountain
by Briley Whitman

I rode on a bike
To take a hike
I went to a mountain
And drank from a fountain
I rode to the top
Then drank a pop
I hustled 'cause of a bear
But it was very rare

What Is Purple?
by Kira Granberg

Purple is amethyst,
Pure and proud,
Purple is pretty,
Like tulips that grow out of the ground.
Purple is a graceful butterfly in the sky.
Purple is soft,
Purple is slow,
Purple is comfortable.

Never Give Up
by Steven Eliass

Creeping through the dark night,
Climbing a mountain with an incredible height,
Running down with a great fright,
Looking for the prey with an anxious sight.
Finding a lot of trees in its way,
Stopping for a moment to get water by the bay,
Moving in the dark with no sun ray,
Still wondering how to find its precious prey.
Is it not the time to give up yet!
But with having its goal already set,
Catching the prey is its aim, I bet,
So, no sleep before the goal is met.
Opening wide its ears, looking front and rear,
Focusing on its target, the way is clear,
Everything is now set, taking slow steps near,
Out of nowhere, the predator will appear.
Hurray, finally catching its prey.
It is time to celebrate, relax, enjoy and lay.
What a great feeling to say;
Never give up is a lesson for every day.

April Fools' Day
by Samantha Simmons

April Fools' Day is a time for pranks
Some people find it fun
Set up your pranks and get ready
But sometimes all people can come up with is a pun.
April Fools' Day can be fun if you don't get pranked
Most people try to avoid being in trouble and say, "Oh it was a joke!"
A lot of people get surprised by a toy snake
Try to annoy someone by a poke poke.
April Fools' Day is funny
I mean, April Fools' Day is a day for laughing
This year it's the same day as Easter
You should hire someone to do the photographing.
April Fools' Day is awesome
Try to prank your pet if you want to
There are so many pranks to choose from
Use some fake dog poo.
April Fools' Day lasts for 24 hours
Hide a toy snake in a toilet
Yell, "Ha Ha Ha!"
Tell your victim don't avoid it.

Heaven
by Blake Beebe

I'm lost in time
No one to show me the way
He took me by the hand
He showed me the way
The way to Heaven
I'm happy now
That I'm in Heaven
God is with me
Now that I'm in Heaven
Thank you God for this
You are my Savior
I love you God
You saved me
From a life of despair
God, you showed me happiness
This is the way of life
My prayers go out to you
God, you are the way
Heaven is paradise
God is life

Questions
by Callie Paxton

In the world there is a person named Callie, she is small but important.
Her character cares and doesn't, her character loves and doesn't,
character helps and doesn't.
She can feel herself not grasping something she needs to.
She wonders what it is and when she starts thinking it gets deep.
What if the world is just a game?
What if she is just a pawn that hasn't been played?
Is she really real?
Or is she something that doesn't have a deal?
Is she a slave playing in someone's grasp?
Or is she free playing in the grass?
Whatever it is she might one day know.
Can she live to ever know?
She hopes to know.
Is she evil or nice?
Is she the fire or the ice?
Is she cold or warm?
Is she special after all?
She can't figure it out, but she has an answer to the last question.
Yes.

The Yard
by Tayah Hilton

The loud animals.
I see mice and birds.
I touch the bark.
I taste the sour apples.
The banging and hammering everywhere I go.
The sour apples me and my brother pick.

Party Hat
by Emma Seefeld

A party hat is a cone-shaped hat.
It can be worn for sorrow or happiness.
But whatever your feelings,
Make sure the real part of what you're celebrating
Is the new year that God has given you!

I Am I
by Logan Roark

I am I, You are You, Dragons are They, and Mammals are too.
I wish I could fly but I am I, and Humans can't fly.
I am I, You are You.
Dragons are They and Mammals are too.
I wish I was You and You were ME
Because I don't think You really see, that I am Me.

Jesus and the Tree
by Jesus Rodriguez

Jesus went outside and climbed up a tree.
He didn't want to get down so he didn't do a thing.
He didn't do it for cake,
And not even pancakes!
Finally Jesus came down from the high tree,
And when he got down he got a sip of tea.

The Test
by Colton Stalker

I'm on the bus sitting and waiting and waiting
I see my class door, I'm looking at the floor
I sit at my desk, waiting for the test
I see the test, looks like a mess
I flip a page, it looks like a maze
I'm halfway through, it took so long I can see the moon

My Dogs
by Emma Pitts

Ranger
fast, cute
drinking, eating, running
home, dog, home, dog
eating, sleeping, eating
slow, brown
Sophie

Moonlight
by Centra A. Carter

It shines bright
It shines every night
You see it every night when you sleep
Moonlight, moonlight
You shine very bright.

Yellow
by Madison Sanders

Yellow feels like a rubber ducky
Yellow tastes like a lemon
Yellow smells like a sunflower
Yellow sounds like a chicky
Yellow looks like a banana

Blue
by Caitlynn Serrer

Blue feels wet like the dark sea.
Blue tastes like the sweetest cotton candy.
Blue smells like a delicious blueberry waffle.
Blue sounds like the waves hitting the shore.
Blue looks like the big sky.

Sad-Happy
by Khloe Downing

Sad
Trouble, Disappointment
Frowning, Crying, Heartbreaking
Heartbroken, Miserable, Excited, Cheerful
Dancing, Hoping, Laughing
Friends, Family
Happy

Freedom For a Girl
by Madelyn Bland

Once a girl wanted to be free
So she even climbed a tall tree
Just to get a view
Of her life brand-new
"It would make me happy," said she

Dinosaurs
by Issabella Miles

Dinosaurs, dinosaurs big and small.
Dinosaurs, how I love them all.
They can be herbivores.
They can be carnivores.
And most of all they can be omnivores.
But you can't stop my love of Dinosaurs.

Baking
by Kiersten C.

I love to bake
that's what I do
can I take your order
can I bake, book me, know that
I will bake for you.
I bake like a star, starting fashion
I bake like a hero, it's my passion
I bake for anyone, ask Uncle Tom
I even baked for my teachers,
my pastor and my mom.
I love to bake, I do, I do
Baking is what I love to do.

Paper
by Jeanna Rall

Going inside paper.
It's flat and smooth.
It's speckled in the light.
Striped with blue lines.
Perhaps a blank piece of paper.
I think paper is very interesting.
I do not know if other people like paper as much as me.
It's white on the inside.
The stories that we write on them are huge to them.
Maybe the photos that we write on them become real life.
I wish I was paper.

Dancing
by Lauren Rudolph

Daring dreams
Artistic moves
Never stop
Character to learn
In attention
Never fear
Greatest sport

Me
by Tay'Nyja Smith

Talented little girl is
Amazing to this
Young world, which will
Never get me down.
You are
Just
Amazing the way you are!

Beauty
by Arlis Spotted

Butterflies fly beautifully.
Eagles are beautifully in the light.
Always beautiful.
U.S.A. is beautiful.
The water is beautifully in the sunlight.
You can be beautiful too.

Majestic Peacock
by Abigail Wheeler

The peacock waits silently
He waits until the right moment
Suddenly his tail feathers spread
Like a rainbow bursting through the clouds
Prancing like a horse
The peacock shows his feathers in the sunlight
And they glisten, as though they are diamonds
He closes his tail feathers
They drag on the ground when he prances
Then he stops
And starts waiting
Silently
Until the right moment

Animals
by Avery Adams

I saw a horse running in the sun
It was beautiful.
I smelled a deer tasting some berries
I heard this sound, it said meow
It was a bobcat
It didn't sound mean.
I saw a deer
I walked up to it and touched it
It was really soft.
I saw a peacock, it was really pretty.
I saw another horse
It was running in water.

Poetry
by Giselle Valenzuela-Barron

Aaaah, poetry, like a twinkle in the sky.
When I'm wide awake, oh wait,
that one is for the dream.
Poetry, when I see you it's like looking
at a bubble of imagination and
maybe a tint of blue. But poetry you,
you are something that was new to me.
I've heard of you before but, now
you are my true love and I
love to just write poetry.
Thank you for becoming a new part
Of my life.

Pets
by Abdul-Rehman Zafar

I have two cats that I like to pat.
Their names are Recees and Purmrose
I like to call Purmrose "Fluffy McFluffins"
They both are four and go through my door.
At the vet, my pet didn't want to be shaved.
My pets don't have toys about,
they think catching birds is a great sport.
Once they played a lot and they almost fought.
One time they took a shower
and in there they started to cower
They are friends, they are sisters
one's a walker and one's a sitter.

Winter
by Evan Sellers

I looked out the window
To a world filled with beauty.
Where snowflakes fell gracefully,
Like lazy white leaves
Spiraling with the wind.
The snow; a white blanket on the ground.
The gentle wind
Rushing through the town,
Whispering sleepy words into all the houses.
The trees are preparing for a long, long sleep.
It is winter.

Which Book Will I Pick?
by Kiernin Yongue

Which book will I pick? Which book will I pick?
It's almost time for lunch, so I better make it quick.
Will I pick a book about fairy tales, or sailing ships at sea?
Or will I pick a little book, about my A B C's?
Will I pick a futuristic book that tells me how to fly,
Or will I pick a zombie book that tells me how to survive?
Will it be big? Will it be small?
Will it be short? Will it be tall?
Will it be old? Will it be new?
I can't find the perfect one to choose.
I can't pick, because I love them all!

Dear Basketball
by Hadley Heiland

Dear Basketball,

How do you bounce so high?
When I only fly up in the air.
How do you sink into the basket?
Do the people ever yell touchdown?
When you go into the goal.
Do you ever get sick?
Do you have little bumps on you?
Do you ever get laid on or as people call it, tackled?

Sincerely, Football

PS. Call me back when you have a chance.

Together
by Brandon A.C. Martin

You are my mom
I am your son
when we're together
I feel like we're doing nothing but fun :-)

I Am
by Penelope Nelson

I am older.
I am faster.
I am taller.
I am stronger.
I am going to have a good day!

In the Mountains
by Landon Pablo

In the mountains
I can smell the trees.
And, see the shade of the tall trees.
I drive with the wind blowing cold air.
And, no music, just the birds.

Freddie
by Noah Zachodny

There once was a frog named Freddie.
Married to a frog named Betty.
They had many kids
Who played with the pigs.
Whose names were Mary and Teddy.

Let's Play Some Ball
by Gianna Passuccio

Bravery
Amazing
Sportsmanship
Keep working
Effort
Take it up
Bouncing the ball
Active
Learn from your mistakes
Listen to the refs

Love
by Adam E.T. Martin

Roses are red
Violets are blue
You love me and
I love you

Morning
by Kaley Salameh

I heard loud chirping
I thought, Yay! It's morning now!
It may be bad that
it is morning but I had
no sleep last night so I'm glad

Birds
by McKinley Criswell

Owl
silent, quick
flying, eating, looking
hovering silently at night, being noisy all around
talking, munching, flapping
loud, colorful
Parrot

Vincent van Gogh
by Eliza Tureck

Van Gogh entered the world in Holland -1853
Impressionism style, bright and festive colors, he adored
Needing higher quality education, sent to a boarding school at age 11
Cut off chunk of ear after a violent fight,
     then gave it to a local woman outside
Eugenie Loyer he loved, though no affection returned
No one noticed his paintings while he lived
Tried to earn a living as teacher, preacher, bookseller, and art dealer

Violently outraged, due to mental illness, he shot himself
Arrived at death's door in France -1890
Near his last days, he painted Wheatfield of Crows

Giving and receiving letters from his brother, Theo,
     inspired The Postman, Arles
Only lived to be 37
Growing better skills at art, he jumped around art schools to test his limits
Helping us learn about Vincent's life,
     we read letters he sent to his brother, Theo

Soccer
by Elly Reed

Super awesome
Outstanding
Crushing it
Coolest thing ever
Energetic
Rad

Dogs-Cats
by Bryce Dunn

Dogs
fun, cute
barking, jumping, running
goldie, beagle, tiger, lion
hissing, scratching, eating
licker, orange
Cats

Beauty
by Eleazar Spotted

Butterflies fly in the meadow
Eagles fly beautiful in the sky
Ants guard the Queen to make life
Use God's blessing to help you
The poor needs help from you
You are God's child - Amen!

Bacon
by Finn Haffey

Best meat ever.
Awesome taste.
Coolest smell.
One of a kind.
Nuclear explosion of awesomeness in my mouth.

Friendship Is Like a Season
by Delaney Mincey

Friendship for a reason, friendship is for a season,
friendship is like a lifetime full of golden seasons.
Summer, spring, winter, fall, our friendship continues through it all.
March, June, September, December
friends go by while the seasons fly.

Pride In America
by Abbigale Little

Pride in America sounds like people who listen.
It tastes like melted caramel on a Rice Krispy Treat.
Pride in America feels like the softness of a fluffy cat.
It looks like the flag.

Track
by Heather Haskins

Triple jump
Relay
All day
Catch the baton
Keep it up!

Love
by Bubbie Brown

Love connects us all
Beating hearts and twinkling eyes
Each day of our lives
The emotion love is sweet
like a chocolate candy treat.

Untitled
by Tomas Leal Arqueros

Games are
amazing sources of
magic. They can be
electronic. They can have multiple
sizes.

Lake
by Hanah Rahmatullah

Cool lake mists and dancing sunbeams
Throw rainbows on the gently rippling surface,
And foaming tongues lick slick pebbles
With a smooth flowing motion.
The shimmering blue expanse is unbroken
Except for mallard ducks floating serenely above.
Minnows dart just out of reach
Among green films of algae.
Pale pinks and vivid oranges color the dusky sky,
Reflecting off the cerulean mirror.
Then stars decorate the calm lake with a glowing orb of moon.

3rd Place

Violet Kinsey

Sunrise
by Violet Kinsey

A stardust-sprinkled sky upon the light of dawn's next day
An elegance upon it takes bad feelings all away
The ruby red and primrose pink upon a painted ocean
While all the wisps of clouds perform an orchestra of motion
The heart of colors new and old that forms a sweet surprise
As peaking over mountaintops comes a fresh and bold sunrise
That sweeps the golden rivers with a beauty of the glimmer
That brings the world close to life with shine and gleam and shimmer.
Crystal days of sunlit stars upon a looking glass
Its deepened face stares down upon the city as days pass
The blue bowl of the sky that brings to all days stars and such
Silhouettes of moon and sun seem close enough to touch
With glowing sense of confidence and lacking of despair
Its voice is calm and comfortable like drumbeats on the air
A silver link, a whispered voice, no pain upon the land
As they're showered with the sunlight
and the warmth of sunshine's hand
By dreams there's many all to spare, by day there's only one
The love and hope that it can bring, the unique and the rising sun.

2nd Place

Ana McCallum-Moore

And I Learn
by Ana McCallum-Moore

The sun on my back,
The dewdrops on leaves,
The breath of the wind,
Teaches me.
The smell of freshly cut grass,
The song of a bird,
The babbling of a brook,
Teaches me,
The spray of a waterfall,
The path of a river,
The ripples on a lake,
They teach me,
And I learn.

**1st
Place**

Brayden Rice

Brayden is a very active honor roll student,
who lists English, Art, and Math
as his favorite subjects.
In addition to writing and drawing,
he enjoys many sports,
including soccer, basketball and lacrosse.
Great work, Brayden!

Success
by Brayden Rice

Every morning, I tell myself, to always try my best,
As long as I didn't give up,
the day will be a success.
Don't measure yourself to others,
because there is only one of you,
You might be good at things,
that others cannot do.
They may do things better than you,
but you always have to try,
When you practice, you will succeed,
the limit is the sky.
If you see someone is struggling,
you should always help them out,
By being a friend when they are down,
you could take away their doubt.
At the end of the day, if I've made you believe,
The day has been a success, and good things you'll achieve.

Division II

Grades
6-7

Summer
by Dylan MacDonald

The fresh summer air
breezes through the sky
as the sun blazes down.

Am I Happy?
by Joshua Diamond-Walls

I feel strange, I feel weird
Am I happy or filled with fear?
Am I happy, am I sad
Am I wacky, am I sad?
My feelings are so mixed up
Am I mad at my brother
Am I sad because of my mother
Is this why I'm wacky?
Is that why I'm happy?
Am I truly happy!?
Am I happy?

Choose Equality
by McKenna Geoghagan

If you had the choice, girls or boys?
Society says we're equal, but problems keep occurring.
We never quite made the change to keep crowds from stirring.
Protests happen nonstop, why do we keep this up?
Can't we just be equal, we're all just people.
Boys and girls are the same species,
why can't we abandon our problems and create treaties?
Stop inequality, increase coequality.
Now, if you had the choice, girls, boys, or both?

Change Her
by Fiona Jenkins

He, Him! words that made Joanie want to throw up.
She was so done with all of the people in her life
calling her by these dreaded words.
Alexander! a name that created scars on her wrists.
It was the name that was decided for her at birth,
a name that would bring her so much pain.
Handsome! a word that tempted her unhealthy eating habits.
A word people would think made her feel better.
Oh how they were wrong.
Masculine! oh how horrible that word was to her.
If only you knew how it would haunt her for eternity.

A Haiku For Change
by Campbell Scharer

Humans have control
So we think, but we thought wrong
Save the biosphere

The Race
by Whitney Thielen

Running
Like lightning speed
Diving
Round barrels one, two, three
Going home
Hair and mane flowing in the wind
Dust
Exploding under our feet
Racing
Against the clock
Mind
Competitive and eager
Slowing
Make one more loop
After the timer
Wonderful
The feel of winning and speed

Life In Me
by Leah Willis

My tears are dry, my heart is full
The world is great, but is getting dull.
My surroundings are beautiful
But one day I'll go
To a better place without sorrow
Where the streaming water flows.
But I'm still here so don't let go
I am real but no one knows.
But when you stop you will see
The beauty that surrounds me.
At night you will hear me
Dancing, singing, and running around
But don't be sad my friend, don't be down.
See me for what I am
Love and beauty that lies within.
For all these things can belong to you
Smiles, giggles, and laughter out loud
Something to cherish, something to do.

Plagiarism
by Kai Winchester

Roses are red
Violets are blue
I copied this
And so should you.

Deforestation
by Braden Garcia

Roses are red
Violets are blue
I would like to save the trees
And I think you should too
Although deforestation isn't helping
There are things that people can do
Like reducing paper waste
Or not wasting sample cups for a simple taste
Deforestation is a serious problem
You can talk to people about it, tell 'em
"Wanna save our world, cut less trees
So that we and our future generations can see
The future that's great
Where you don't have to wait
Ten thousand years for 1 pencil because there
Are plentiful trees and oxygen
That you can even hold in a pen."

Rain
by Jaiden Lundell

Rain is not always sadness, dripping, waiting, feeling, but happiness
Rain is the creation of God
His tears of joy because
of his beautiful creation that glimmers
In the light of the moon and the sun
never not a time for
His wonderful tears to
splash onto your face
The beautiful trickling silence
is interrupted by beautiful
roars of thunder
vacating the drip and the drops
Flashing cannot be predicted
Striking and piercing the sound barrier
With a sonic boom the ground shakes leaving
Behind a trail of blazing fire and static electricity,
scattered throughout the land.

Plant's Life
by Harlow Decunto

First you start a little seed.
Then you grow up.
Then you grow some more,
Till you become a tree galore.
Then you make more of you
And start all over again.

My Best Friend
by Shekinah Weary

They call him a man's best friend
He'll be there until the end
He's there when I'm mad
He licks my face when I'm sad
When my heart is broken
With words unspoken
He opens my heart with his key
And I feel the love he has for me
He always makes me laugh and smile
I hope he's there when I walk down the aisle
And when my children arrive
He'll be right by my side
When I grow old
He'll be there to console
Cooper, I love you
And I know you love me, too

No One
by Courtney Taylor

There is so much wrong with the world
But no one seems to see,
That boy being treated like an outsider,
And that girl being teased.
All the people see are criminals and crooks,
Because everyone overlooks,
That grown man crying,
And that special woman dying,
Those boys caught up in a fight,
Hoping a fist doesn't take flight.
For once I wish someone would take action …
Join the boy, stop the teasing,
bring happiness to someone's life, or maybe even save one
Just bring an end to the violence,
to the threats and to the debts.
Even the smallest changes make a big difference.

Eggs
by Seina Munguia

Eggs, so delightful.
You can scramble them and boil them, put them on toast too.
You can drop them on someone's head and have a laugh.
Eggs, so delicious I eat them almost every day for breakfast.
Sometimes I have them on pizza.
Ohh, how I love eggs

Ode To Rex
by Annie Badaruddin

Look at his happiness.
Look at his silky soft fur.
His eyes like glass.
His voice like silence.
I saw him having fun,
I knew he was the one.
I loved his little face.
He likes to play chase.
I hear him bark.
He was my spark.
His name is Rex.
He isn't very complex.
He is black and brown.
I love him to sundown.
With his brown eyebrows,
You always hear his bow wows.

Stars
by Madison Knoth

The stars shining bright above
Twinkling in the sky,
Dazzling me when I look up,
Right away catching my eye.
Shining light down on the heavens,
They sparkle, every which way,
Brightening everything in their path,
Stunning, I might say.
Bright as the sun themselves,
They brighten up my day,
Sparkling from up above,
Shining over the open bay.
The stars are lovely, beautiful things,
Brightening the land below,
They sparkle, dazzle, and brighten the world,
Oh, how they shine just so.

The Night Sky
by Seth Wainwright

The moonlit sky shone like a Van Gogh painting placed in the heavens
It was bereft of the problems of our everyday lives,
yet awash with stars
A jet black shade
blended with the subtle fog surrounding us
The moon smiled at the Earth, as it stared into the ocean
and all of its creatures
Yet, we look forward to dawn

Going Green To Keep This Earth Clean
by Zoey Hensley

Going green to keep the water clean
a leading hand can keep the animals clean
Pollution is bad enough
and even when the atmosphere is involved
on its way air quality is pollution's way
toxins and chemicals down the drain
the animals are just not safe
water is a resource we all need to have
without water we would die in a flash
Earth will die out and have no time for land
Earth would not have time to be green
and blue seas are polluted, fish are all dying fast
Pollution happening, animals can hardly breathe
So lend a hand, help as much as you can
Pollute again and think what could end

Never Again
by Allie Stowers

The butterflies in your stomach before you enter the ring, never again
The late nights clipping your animal before the show, never again
Grabbing your lucky show whip and brush before you enter the ring
Never again
The last last minute, never again
Family standing behind you the whole way you enter the ring, never again
The anxiety that you have everything ready, never again
The judge announcing your name, never again
The slap happening, never again
Stepping foot in the show ring, never again
How hard it was just to load the crazy animal, never again
Tears filling your eyes that it was your last show, never again
Saying goodbye to your favorite show animal, never again
Family yelling your name, never again
Funny how all your show animals go to the same place

My Family
by Jalisha M. Robles

My family smells like
an ocean breeze, warm, trustworthy, comforting
My family feels like
socks, drama free carpet, wood floors that are rough, but sturdy
My family looks like
a thousand dollars in arms' reach–
they're worth the world just waiting to start again
My family is just the world

They Don't Frighten Me At All
by Camryn Chick

They don't frighten me at all
Lions feeding on their prey
Monsters hiding in the doorway
They don't frighten me at all
They don't frighten me at all
Freaky clowns in the night
Scary dogs that bite
They don't frighten me at all
They don't frighten me at all
Creepy, crawly snakes
When cars don't hit their brakes
They don't frighten me at all
They don't frighten me at all
Not at all, not at all
They don't frighten me at all

A Demon In Disguise
by Grace Pendley

I feel emotions of a wide variety.
I am no longer a child with an innocent smile.
I can only feel the anxiety.
This is why I want love, even if for only a little while.
I face this cold darkness alone.
I have long lost my faith.
I have sins that no one can atone.
This life is only a curse, only a wraith.
I fear I will be hurt, but yet I still want support.
I do not need to hear another accusation.
I have been hurting for too long in life lacking comfort.
This is my only statement, a dimmed and dying voice's last declaration.
I wish I did not have to end my life before it had even begun,
but I am plagued by the demon, depression.
This is my crying confession.

Soldier's Bravery
by Bryton Allard

I am a soldier, do you know me?
I left my home, my friends, and family.
I am not perfect, but I am strong.
I will try to give you a place to "carry on".
For anyone in need, I will defend,
Even until the bitter end.
As you sleep in your niche,
Please know I have your six.

The Girl In the Mirror
by Briana Powell

What do you think when you look in the mirror?
Do you think,
I wish I could be prettier,
Or, do you think,
I wish I could be skinnier?
The girl in the mirror was prettier,
And skinnier,
If only I could be her,
She's the girl in the mirror.
She's the one with more self-esteem,
The one who's better than me,
The one I'll never be.
The one the world knows,
The one who's never afraid to show,
That she's the girl in the mirror.

Mornings At My House
by Iliana Louis

I wake to the familiar sounds of family quarreling
as the TV hangs low in the background, waiting to be noticed.
I hear the drumming of small feet racing towards my door.
The door bursts open to reveal a great big smile plastered on my challenger's face.
She began her journey across the battlefield littered with deadly mounds of stench
embedded clothing and spiky Legos which seem to migrate through rooms.
You can see the determination bursting with every step,
as she eagerly rushes forward,
bubble wand in one hand, half eaten chip in the other.
At last, she reaches the boss level.
She raises her bubble wand and chants the sacred spell:
"Na-na! Wake up! It's time to eat!"
And with that, my curse is lifted.
I take my savior's hand and we head back, ready to conquer our next adventure:
chocolate chip pancakes!

Sea Turtles
by Anna Buonocore

Rocky like a dinosaur,
Underwater fins do really soar, munching on jellyfish galore,
As easy as counting to four
Slow but fast when needed, they truly can't be beat,
As they play in forests of seaweed,
They are always greeted,
Quiet and tranquil but unpredictable,
Blend in always waiting,
Some things go by so fast but they sit, not missing a second of it,
But if they do they never have a fit

My Dad
by Trinidy Boyce

My dad! My hero! Best friend forever!
Loves me when I'm happy, loves me when I'm sad
Strong, courageous, funny, super clever
He's here to help me in good times and bad
Guiding me with his knowledge- love- advice
No matter the problem he's by my side
For all his kids he has made great sacrifice
In all that he does in his heart and pride
Enjoys: outdoors, nature, mountains, rivers
Fishing, hunting, exploring new places
He says what he means and always delivers
Never wanting to fall from his graces
No other dad compares to mine ever
My dad, my hero, best friend forever

The Final Day
by Nasir A. Zaidi

Today was the day. The final day. The day of the end.
As I walked by, I saw people cry, which began to put tears in my eyes.
There was the pole. The pole of doom. And there they tied me up.
The man stood in front of me. I asked, "How long will this be?"
He said, "Ein paar sekunden [a few seconds]."
And I put my head down in shame, as the people cried out my name,
which made me feel even worse.
They yelled, "Spare him, spare the hero!"
And they yelled back, "Nein halt die Klappe [no shut up],"
and they became as silent as a mouse.
They yelled, "Tote ihn [kill him]!"
And I looked at my house, my family, and my friends.
Then I heard a loud bang, and the beautiful world turned to darkness.
Then I saw light. And in that light I saw him.

The Little Blackbird
by Torri Vanderhoff

This Brewer Blackbird is so fantastic
I just feel like it is plastic
I feel sorrow like this bird
I just say nothing– no word
It is like me, sad and dramatic
But I am just a huge fanatic
This bird can be peaceful
But its lunch is not a beetle
They came from western North America
But mine I might name Erica

A Splash of Fun
by Emily Brevig

The ocean never-ending
with a light sun reflection
palm trees swaying with the wind
Warm sand making your feet tingle
playing beach volleyball
hitting, passing, setting, serving
The ball going, going
running, pass
diving, miss
Time to play in the blue ocean
running from waves
up, down
slap, waves hit the beach
The ocean never-ending

Trees.
by Grace Touring

Land, oh so lovely, now perished.
Cool shadows are now a burning light.
The Eden that we once cherished
Is now a very repulsive sight.
It's heating up, temperatures rising.
"Toxic gases" left in the air.
When will the animals start dying,
And how much more can we bear?
Living things are falling,
And do we even mind at all?
The elegant furniture we're shopping
Made from green life, that was so tall.
What more will die for us,
Until we soon start to fall.

Human Impact
by Devin Conner

The world was created 4.5 billion years ago
Then we came and initiated the process of erosion
We cut down trees in order for our people to grow
We polluted the air which began to make polar caps unfrozen
We're destroying the animals of the ocean
We just don't care about the environment
This lifestyle of ours is a fatal notion
We have started to kill animals' environments on "accident?"
Help us get together and fix this man-made problem
If we change things maybe it will make other ecosystems blossom

Tick Tock Writers Block
by Audrey Swingle

The minutes slowly stretched on,
Each longer than the last.
Seconds turned to minutes,
Minutes to hours.
The clock ticked tauntingly
And its cold, metal hands
Seemed to move achingly slow.
A piece of notebook paper sat
Innocently empty alongside
Multiple crumbled sheets.
A lone pencil lay on the floor,
Long since forgotten,
Just like the poem
That hadn't been written.

Into the Storm
by Rhys Miley

Into the storm, my day was nice and warm
Until the monster started to form
Into the storm, it comes my way
Taking all the happiness away
Into the storm, the rain smashes against the ground
Seemingly causing all life to drown
Into the storm, the wind gets terribly loud
As it moaned and shrieked and howled
Into the storm, the thunder's deafening roar
Shakes my house's roof and floor
Into the storm, it starts to go
And in its place comes a rainbow
Into the storm, we help one another
It's all ok, we have each other

Water Pollution
by Diya Patel

Water, water, it's good for you
It must be used wisely, can't be overused
We will need it today and tomorrow, too
Don't use too much, there won't be enough for you
Don't abuse it then no one can use it
To wash their hands, to clean their hair
There will be none left for us to spare
Water is a gift so don't waste it
Turn it off when you're done
There will be enough for everyone

Ode To Odyssey, the Boat
by Carly Reed

Oh Odyssey,
You're my all in crew,
I can't even think of you
Not being in my practices,
People think that you are,
An old man trying to swim.
But that makes you wise,
And you know the twists and turns,
Of the river.
And you guide me through every obstacle
Knowing that you'll keep me safe
Oh, Odyssey, Oh Odyssey,
I can never picture me,
Without you at crew.

Matron of Purity
by Juliette Puig

Lady Widow beyond the street,
Whose house we do not speak.
With chipped brown paint and wooden seats,
That rock and creak.
Moonlight glares down upon her house buried in the West,
Yet the burden she bears brings me to rest.
For her prosperity and choice perished in flames,
Along with her dearest and she is to blame.
For she harnesses the guilt and transparency of one's heart,
She was a matron of purity,
Now she leaves shattered parts.
Across the street there lies a pond,
With baby blue birds that do not speak
Just like Lady Widow beyond the street.

The Days of My Youth
by Isabella Pica

As the water flows back to shore
It makes me think more and more
Back to the days of my prime
Like a newborn chicken in springtime
How I remember even the worst of days
But the happier ones keep me in a daze
Sunday dinner with the family, playing with friends
But now I've realized even the best days end
Though. Now I know those days are gone
Throughout. My memories they will forever live on.

I Believe
by Tessa Stokes

I believe in faith.
You have to have faith to believe in yourself.
I believe in hope.
You need hope in your life.
I believe in family.
You need family to be happy.
I believe in integrity.
It is good to be honest.
I believe in teamwork.
It is great to work with someone else.
I believe in love.
Love is a powerful thing.
I believe in friends.
Friends help you in bad situations.

School
by Blakelyn Tucker

When I wake up
I go to school
It is a little hard for me when I get there.
It's not quite so bad when I study spelling
But I am often troubled by the words I don't know;
The lessons I can't understand
And the other things that don't make sense.
My favorite subject is science.
I like reading too.
Math is fun but sometimes it is hard.
When I wake up
I go to school.
It is a little hard for me when I get there,
But I keep trying and never quit.

The Eagle
by Alessandro Benedito

Soaring in the day
Resting in the night
Swooping through the countryside
An everlasting symbol of might
Roosting in the trees
Flying with ease
Trying to rest
For the bird is the nation's very best
America's symbol
Is not an easy task
For the American eagle
Is our very best

The Birds Live In the Trees
by Prince Williams

The birds live in the trees
I hear them tweeting all day
They come and go with ease
The birds live in the trees
The birds live in the trees
I watched them fly from limb to limb
As the limbs move in the breeze
The birds live in the trees
The birds live in the trees
They fly from tree to tree
Sometimes they even fly over me
As leaves from the trees fall free
The birds live in the trees

The Essence of Me
by Kate Wynkoop

There are mountain ranges where the trees grow high,
Through seasons of changes and dusty blue sky.
The mountains protrude out of mist. In the air, a chill,
The clouds and land tenderly kissed where cool winds bring a thrill.
The hills recede and rise, the ground collapses into shape,
Sunbeams blazing from misty skies, upon mountainsides red-rock draped.
The fresh, crisp air reddens the nose, with country aroma-filled wood,
Distant valleys seen as far as it goes, beyond where cliff sculptures stood.
Frigid waters, like ice to the touch, where grass blankets warm the land,
With splashes of white, gold and such,
the peaceful Smokey's substantially stand.
The beauty within them calls my name, the taste of thrill and tranquility,
The passion of my heart, I cannot tame. Come discover the essence of me.

My Locker
by Grayson Christie

I use my locker
I can store important things
I use my binders

A Horrible Day Doesn't Frighten Me
by Addie Thorson

A horrible day doesn't frighten me.
They can be ignorable or not.
They don't make me mad.
They don't make me sad.
The bullies who tackle me down.
The people who spin me around.
Those people definitely don't scare me!
The snakes that try to bite.
Despite the fact they do try to attack.
Going to class and getting side-tracked.
Then getting called back after class.
Why should I be frightened?
A horrible day doesn't frighten me!
I can always make a horrible day a good day.
But I can never make a good day a bad day.
It's just one day, how could I be frightened?
A horrible day doesn't frighten me one bit!

Garage Sale
by Max Thallemer

Over spring break I went to a garage sale.
It was hard to find a garage even though it was a garage sale.
But it was hard to find someone selling their junk.
But another man's garbage is another man's treasure.
This is not all rainbows, there is a bad part, a good part, and a lucky part.
This is the bad part and the lucky part.
I went with my older brother looking for garages that were open.
We went to the front of our neighborhood
and saw the two most glamorous vases. I bought them both for a dollar.
One glass and one metal
my brother took the metal one and drove off on his bike to my house.
I took the glass one, driving with one hand on my bike
and my other hand holding the glass vase I took off.
This is where the lucky part comes in.
I could not get hold of the brakes in time so I ran out of control and fell off.
I looked at the vase and there were no scratch marks on it.
I safely got home with the vase, put flowers in it and gave it to my mom.

Alaskan Wilderness
by Breelynn McCaffree

In northern Alaska,
the wind howls and the wolves howl along with it,
as the northern lights dance in the night sky.

Depression
by Gabrielle Farmer

My stomach aches, my ribs on display
Yet I refuse to eat to no one's dismay
I'm too fat to be seen,
Yet you say I'm as thin as a pole,
But I won't believe your lies
I'm ugly, I'm broken
There is no fixing what cannot be fixed
I stay awake at night,
My thoughts eat me up inside
Yet you don't know and you won't know
I force a smile every day
So that I might seem ok
And it works;
You don't have to deal with my problems only yours
And I'll be out of your hair soon
With these cuts on my arms and pills in my hand
One day I'll see you again

Escape the Opposite
by Alyssa Messina

The compass points north, I go south,
Then it points east, I go west,
Wherever I was told to go,
The wind blows me the opposite way,
But no not this time, my feet are grounded,
The people follow, people chase, people watch,
They hover over me,
They criticize every move I make,
No one cares what I feel or see,
Not long until I can't take,
The rudeness, the pain, the pain of words that go into my ear,
The words need to get out,
They need to escape from the jail that is my mind,
The metal bars of my thoughts won't break,
I feel like my life is at stake,
get me out, break me free.
Help me escape the opposite.

My Rabbit
by Drew Gaczkowski

My rabbit is white
He likes to fight
The rabbit likes to eat and sleep
Then he likes to repeat
And he does this with all his might

Reflecting In Paradise
by Christopher Zizzo

At the beach, by myself,
Having a peaceful day,
Looking at all the life,
Thinking about my way.
Having a peaceful day.
Looking at the shells in the sand,
Thinking about my way.
Such a beautiful day.
Looking at the shells in the sand.
The sun rays tingle my skin.
Such a beautiful day.
Bright on the outside and within.
The sun rays tingle my skin.
Happiness on the highest shelf.
Bright on the outside and within.
At the beach, by myself.

Rain's Journey
by Eli Greer

People assume when the sky's cool blue,
The day will turn out grand.
But when the sky's dark gray, they say
The day will turn out bland.
When the rain falls like cold tears,
The children stay inside.
They walk within their walls and halls,
Their boredom cannot hide.
Some enjoy the light downpours.
It transforms the corn strong yellow.
When Rain goes to the soft green countryside,
It makes him feel quite mellow.
Rain himself is colorless.
But when Rain goes elsewhere,
He leaves a brightly colored path
That ends just on the edge of nowhere.

Football
by Cason Krumm

Sports
Competitive, Competition
Running, Yelling, Catching
"Down, Set ... Hut"
Football

Change
by Christopher Davis

Happiness is not bought
Wars should not be fought
When things don't go your way
Know that things will change
You have your own choice
Now go help people have a voice
Know you are always loved
By your ancestors up above
This world is filled with darkness
You can be the spark upon us
If you start a positive chain reaction
You will start to notice some action
Try to spread good vibes
Maybe others will be just as nice
Now show some pride
And be that guide

The Wonders of the Outdoors
by Benjamin Meitner

The trees waving in the air
And the hibernating friendly bear
With the cool smooth breeze
Flying yellow and black honey bees
It is so majestical out there
All the animals have no scare
With everything they will ever need
Life out there has the feed
All the fish have a blast
Until a fisher throws a cast
Then all the fish scatter
But the bass don't know what's the matter
When a bear comes to grab a bite
All the fish swim in fright
Sometimes you should go explore
The wonders of the outdoors

Pigs
by Sarah-Jean Richart

I may roll around in my filth but at least I'm free,
I see the sun rise oh it gleams,
the water over yonder I will drink it like no others need it,
I am in this pen not leaving,
not one hoof shall touch the ground of the world outside,
rolling around in this mud I will get dirty and will not get washed off,
I am the one who will run free,
trotting over the river stream,
maybe I'll find an apple for me to eat,
I don't need to wait for a human to feed me,
wanting more food I starve in this cage,
wanting out but there is no escape,
from this cage that I shall stay in,
I wish I could leave and be like him,
I run I leap I am free,
I will go out in the world since no one shall stop me,
I will not be feasted on, no one will eat me,
on this chopping board that I lay on,
the knife going swiftly by cutting me apart,
I am no longer in this cage of defeat,
I am free

A Kid Who Struggles
by Eli Walz

There was once a kid
On the outside, he was like everybody else
But that was just what he wanted people to see him as.
He struggled on grades, on friends, on family, on life,
But that doesn't mean he should end it all with a knife.
At school, he had a decent number of friends,
All his friends would help him through the end.
And then he had one friend who helped him realize something,
That listening to music can help if he can sing.
He tried it and loved it,
He loved it so much that he wanted to get out of his pit.
He didn't want to be done anymore,
He wanted to sing, and dance and listen to it more.
Listening to music put him in a good mood,
So, at school, he was going to try to act good.
He got good grades, made new friends, fixed family problems,
He even fixed his happiness, resolving that problem.
In the end, everything worked out,
He had everything he wanted which he had no doubt.
And he lived happily ever after.

Equality
by Tavisha Singh

They say we can be whatever we want,
Without others giving a taunt,
But the ones who shall stay at home are girls,
Do this and that and twirl,
And they say we're trapped in this swirl,
How will this end,
They say everyone can go at their own pace,
Without caring about any race,
But they say you're the wrong color,
And how you're so much duller,
And how you can't be the fuller,
How will this end,
They say we can believe whatever,
And live like this forever,
You believe who,
And some say it can't be true,
Making others feel blue,
How will this end,
It ends with equality

Looking Up At the Stars
by Kinlee Snell

Looking up at the stars
Thinking of all the things they could be
Joy now filling my heart
So beautiful it's like a fantasy
Look up high into the night
So far above our heads
Stars are lighting up the sky
While we are sleeping in our beds
Shooting stars fly by so fast
Competing with each other
Trying not to be very last
At the end laughing with one another
Look up high into the night
So far above our heads
Stars are lighting up the sky
While we are sleeping in our beds
Stars are so beautiful
Painting the sky with light
So bright and wonderful
Always coming out during the night
Sitting and watching them
Loving every moment with my own likeness
Makes me feel like the person I am
Watching them battle with the darkness

The Roller Coaster
by Sofia Adams

It's like you're on a roller coaster
You go up and you go down
You go all around
But then you wait
You sit and wait
And it gets crazy
It goes upside down
And the right side up
But then it gets chill
So, just remember
It's like you're on a roller coaster
going all around

Pirate Ship
by Aubrey Hawley

Screws rust, wood rots, many slivers in my hand
Climb up the ladder, go down the slide
Hurry and get back up before the sharks get us
Look in the distant, dark blue sea
Then Grandma calls us in
For a delicious lunch of Sloppy Joes and punch
Run back out, and climb back up
Save a dolphin and her pup
We sail east and find an island
Release the dolphins in a safe place
Mom calls us in, time to go home
Dolphins saved, memories stay

Approaching Storm
by Lila Milliman

Branches blow bare with the breeze
While they hold on tight to the trees
Waves slam hard on the beach
As teachers try to teach
The grass is brown and dead
And the birds soar overhead
Dark clouds fill the sky
And all of our crops will die
Once the rain begins to pour
As the rain falls more and more
Falling, falling, pitter, patter
The rain falls hard splatter, splatter

Slime Is Mine
by Alayna Williams

Slime, it is mine,
Slime, it is so fine,
Slime, it smells like lime,
Slime, it doesn't take up much time,
Slime, it only costs one dime,
You can put a dime on my slime,
You can do so much with slime,
You might find it so fine,
You can make it fluffy bluffy,
And glossy foxy,
You can also make it crunchy munchy,
And so much more!

Sisters
by Kendall Freeman

For all the years we've shared our lives,
the roof we both lived under,
we'd laugh but we'd also cry,
scared of lightning storms and thunder.
The younger years have gone by fast,
you've went your separate way,
through all the time,
our bond will always remain.
The summer begins the happy times,
the fall leaves start to whisper,
the best friend I'd ever find,
is the one I call my beautiful sister.

One In a Lillian
by Kaylie Johnson

Lillian is a dear friend of mine.
I know her, but I've never met her.
She took her last breath before I took my first.
I've always felt close to her and she's always felt close to cardinals.
I love cardinals.
She watched over my dad, loved my mom.
She knew us before there was an "Us" ...
At least, I hope this is true.
During the worst times, this is what I hold on to.
I keep her word.
Rest in peace, NanaBird.
My full name is Kaylie Lillian Johnson.

The Rain
by Sandra Jenkins

The rain is pouring
The rain is beautiful now
The rain says goodnight

Wind
by Tori Reeves

Leaves moving on trees
Plants are moving in the breeze
Birds flying in wind

Think Before You Throw
by Kiley Wenger

Water once blue in its place,
Turned an odd hue due to haste,
Harming the animals that it once encountered,
But many thought it didn't really matter.
Well now I am here to tell you it does
Because many died that once were loved.
Think before you throw.

Pollution
by Muna Aboushaar

You drink water every day,
You also use it for showers.
But some places don't have clean water today,
And that's because of polluted waters.
Water is essential to all life,
So let's all find a solution
To this major problem that isn't a joke,
Also known as pollution.

Sea Me
by Ashley Artau

See me,
See me,
Why won't you see me?
Is it perhaps the sea in front of your eyes?
Or is it the sight of a million grains of sand?
But may I ask,
If you can see the sea,
Why can't you see me?

Mazzy
by Reef LaGala

Your bark so sweet
Your face so cute
Your soft heartbeat
Your tackle so brute
A sweet Pitbull
You will never be forgotten
Your fur felt like wool
And some wild cotton
But we all come to an end
You will always be in my heart
You were my best friend
Now it's time to restart.

Branding
by Joseph Schiffer

Out in the corral in the hills.
wrestling the biggest calves in the pen.
after they have mothered up in the summer pasture.
dust in my eyes
boots falling apart
sweat dripping down my back
worried mama cows bellering
scared calves
the smell of singed hair fills the air
worming and vaccinating all the calves
fly tags in their ears
turn them out in the summer pasture!

Close-Out
by Barrett Baker

There was sweat in my eyes, and fans everywhere.
The final inning was coming to a close.
The sun was burning my face,
I locked in on the catcher and threw the ball.
As the ball left my hand a rush went through my body
I tried to keep myself calm.
Then the ball flew into the catcher's palm
We did what no one thought that we could
I jumped in the air higher than I ever have before.
That moment will never be forgotten.
It will always be in my core.
Definitely one of the most stressful but successful days of my life.

War
by Olivette Copple

War is
a pitch-black bloodbath
of stories now forgotten.
A thousand
memories
lost within
a single
gunshot.
War is
chaos.
An off-pitched
chorus
screaming
screeching
splintering
splitting
clanking sounds of weapons
and another human being
irreplaceably gone.
Who is the real enemy?

I Know a Girl
by Kaylinn Turney

There's a girl I know
Her head hangs low
Her wrists are scarred, as well as her heart
There's a girl I know
With tears in her eyes
Paints on a fake smile, but they're all lies
There's a girl I know
With a past so dark, as hard, as she tries to forget
It will always leave a mark
There's a girl I know
Cries herself to sleep, scared to go to school
Scared of the bullies that creep
There's a girl I know
That left one day
Without saying goodbye, never even said 'hey'
There's a girl I know with such a kind heart
We've been friends since the very start
If only they'd try to talk to her
Maybe they'd see, how much she meant
To no one but Me

The Total
by Wyatt Thielen

Power wheelie-vroom
Riding the dirt bike
Marking the ground
Hitting jumps
Flying through the air
Stomach rolling
Heart beating
Whop, "Ow," I say
But I get back up again
More jumps
Whop ... Whop ... Whop ...
You total it
I'm thinking nothing can replace Loraine
When am I going to learn?
Then Liberty Mutual calls
And they pay for a brand new one
A shiny red
Black leather seat
Honda XR120
Vroom

Raised Wrong
by Espan Patton

I was raised by the unknown, the never-knowing-where-I-was-going.
The uncertainty of who to turn to. The constant guessing of who to trust.
The mind games, the trusting and then being hurt,
always wondering and never knowing.
I was raised by a lie, the "I'm fine, leave me alone" lie.
The lie to myself that I'm happy, cheerful, full of love not hate
that I was surrounded by the light not the dark,
but it was a lie that I keep telling and never realizing the truth.
I was raised by invisibility. Always trying to hide, slumped over, head down,
never speaking and maybe no one would notice me.
Stuck in the dark, cloudy shadows that I hide in and never getting noticed.
I was raised by the sadness. The never-knowing,
the lying, and the hiding were all caused by sadness.
The crushing-inside-darkness running my life
that's always lingering down inside and never rising.
Always down, never up, always sinking deeper and deeper,
until you hit rock bottom and you think you can't possibly go down but you do,
and that's when you start to hope
that one day you start to go towards the happiness
but it's hard to be happy when all you can manage is a fake smile.

Thoughts On the Miami School Shooting
by Scarlet Harsey

Am I scared?
Am I worried?
Am I prepared?
Should I scurry?
All of these things run through my head,
When all of these students question, "Should I be dead?"
While these parents are worried to death,
Again I think under my breath,
Am I scared?
Am I worried?
Am I prepared?
Should I scurry?
Was there a helper?
Will they be caught?
Why did they do this?
What was their thought?
But the biggest thoughts I continue to think,
Am I scared?
Am I worried?
Am I prepared or should I scurry?

The Girl Underwater
by Evelyn Rittenhouse

There once was a girl with a dream,
Her dream was to venture to the deep,
She knew nothing in the deep would be the same theme.
Tomorrow she will fulfill her dream, but now some sleep.
Today the girl gets ready and all suited up,
And the people before her get dry.
She never realized how scary the ocean was close up,
But she sat down, looked up, and said, "Goodbye."
The girl dives right in and tries to remember,
What her dad told her when she was last in the water.
She goes back to the days of early September.
Her father said he will always watch over his beautiful daughter.
She looked around and started to cry,
She looked at the boat's engine and worries,
As it starts up she wonders why?
She sees the boat start to leave, so she swims and hurries.
The boat is now gone and she's stranded for good.
She knows what's going to happen to her, death.
She will see her father soon, at least she should.
It has been days, so she prays and takes her last breath.

Space Destiny
by Parker Gross

I like to gaze at the stars.
Thinking about how high we'll climb.
Thinking about exploring the galaxy.
It's just a matter of time.
I cannot wait to explore.
To go to space.
Beyond our shores.
Beyond our shores.
We will explore.
Beyond our solar system.
Always wanting to know more.
We will venture to new planets.
And I will want to join the corps.
Like birds we will fly.
Our curiosity will never die.
By traveling we will learn more.
By seeing new worlds with our own eyes.
We will travel with light-speed.
To new galaxies.
We will fulfill our curiosity's needs.

Death
by Peyton Prill

I cannot sleep, I cannot wake
Oh, may Heaven decide my fate
Is this Hell is this Heaven? I am not dead nor am I alive
How is this so, how can I not be alive?
When this is over shall I forever sleep,
Friend of the dead, never to wake
Forever in Heaven, is this my fate?
A man's fate, my fate is to live, to be alive
Wait Heaven, arise from sleep
I wish to wake, to leave the dead
Death, I will not join the dead, dearest fate
Fast I rise, fast I wake, full of life alive
Sleep only tonight's sleep, Heaven one day my Heaven
Will I stay, will I join Heaven? Will my heart stop and will I join the dead
Will I endure my unending sleep, will life or death be my fate?
Oh, God how I want to be alive, from my slumber shall I wake
From my tombstone shall I wake, oh how I want to join Heaven
But how cherished it must be to be alive, shall I see the sun again
or forever watch my tombstone silently with the dead?
Oh, God only you can decide my poor fate ... or will I forever sleep

Rain
by Samuel Gustafson

I let my hand out of the pocket of my jacket,
And let it feel the waterdrops falling from the sky.
The air grows silent in the mist.
I let out a calming sigh,
And let myself bathe in the falling rain.
Walking calmly through the quiet street,
I listen to the sound of falling rain below my feet.
I watch as the world around me becomes calm.
Engulfed by the sound of it.
I raise my umbrella to the sky.
As to shield me from the cold of the water.
My own personal protection.
I think to the past of times of peace,
To the past of times of hopes and dreams.
And think of my times as a child.
When I would play in the puddles,
And sleep under a soft tree covered with raindrops.
As the storm fades away,
I wish to whomever else the storm follows,
They will feel the calming and playful rain.

The Mangroves
by Matthew Zorovich

Caught a redfish, trout, snook, and a jack
Put on some fresh bait and casted it back
My line started bobbing up and down
But then it snapped and it gave me a frown
I got out my tackle box, took out the leader
Then I got my clippers and cut it to half a meter
Then I put on a brand new circle hook
Hoping that I would catch another snook
Right as I put my line in, fish started biting
My rod bent down really far, it was exciting
In the distance I saw it hopping
A tarpon in the waves that were pounding and chopping
It was a couple yards away from the boat
A tarpon with a silvery coat
I got out the scale to find its weight
It weighed 62 pounds, that was really great
We threw the tarpon back in the water
The sun was getting less and less hotter
We headed back home, back into our beds
As the memory of fishing buzzed around in our heads

Which Shall I Choose?
by Sophia Panarese

I'm stuck between two arts I love
But I can only choose just one
Oh help me Lord, you are above
This whole thing's turning to no fun
I could choose band or maybe art
Which do I choose? I'm starting to plea
No one can tear us three apart
I love them both oh can't you see?
One has notes that fill a room
It lets you hear if you're not there
The sound goes through your ear ... zoom
When played right, you get good stares
The other fills a page with lead
Shading away to bring to life
Some people like to paint instead
But I can't bring that on a drive
Tik, tok, tik, tok, the clock goes on
Still seeking for an answer ... day by day
Soon, oh soon, my time will be gone
Then I'll see if I draw or play

The Walk
by Drew Hurley

I walk.
Whoosh goes a car like a red blur around the corner
I stop, stand, stare
Questioning why. Why does the car go by?
I walk a block or two to find the car again speeding down the road,
This time it was different.
There were two so I keep walking
I listen.
Hoot hoot goes two owls in the trees
Rustle rustle goes a silent creature lurking in the bushes.
I wander off the sidewalk into the brush
All is quiet except for the crickets and the frogs singing in the night.
I walk a little farther.
I see a glow.
I wonder what it is and why is it glowing.
They are fireflies on a plain.
I sit down,
I look out into my little town, I see the lonely cars driving around
But here it is peaceful
All is beautiful here.

The Heart of Nature
by Nick Moore

I am the only one left in nature
Which brings me to cry
Happiness is now a stranger
We all live to die
I stand alone in the storm
As I am beaten down by the rain
My depressing thoughts come in a swarm
All I know is pain
My days alone are endless
For those who live in joy
I will always be jealous
Death will never cease to destroy
Being all alone is one of my greatest fears
Saying I'm alone is the biggest lie
Because every night I am reduced to tears
All I can do in the wretched place is cry
It is nearly the end
As I drown closer to death
I will hopefully soon ascend
And I take my final breath.

Fake
by Mikaela Houle

All they did was make her cry.
She realized that and let out a sigh.
She wiped away the tears.
It wasn't worth it to have them here.
All they caused were mascara smears.
"I don't want them anymore," she said,
Yet she couldn't get them out of her head.
She wanted to cut them out,
Yet they kept coming about.
She began to have a lot of doubt.
She began to think,
About the ones who made her cheeks go pink.
They made her happy,
Never made her want to flee.
She knew she loved them dearly.
Find real friends, she thought,
Not ones who make you distraught.
Ones who make you laugh,
Who you feel as though they are your better half.
Just keep your head up high, like a giraffe.

Summertime
by Catherine Coffey

Sunshine shining on my hair
Everywhere I go I have fun
Giving quite a bright glare
Cold sodas by the pool
The time of year with no school
I love summertime
Jokes and games that make me grin
Seeing friends, shouting, "Where have you been!"
Vacations to exotic places
We all have big smiles on our faces
I love summertime
We play until the day is done
Warm days, cool nights
Swim meets and flying kites
I love summertime
Running on the beach
Collecting shells and counting each
Sand in between my toes
This is how my summer goes
I love summertime

The Children of Change
by Lily Demkovich

Long ago, somewhere very far away,
Mother's kin were taken away.
To be sold to the trade, did not bother pleading on their knees,
They only knew that justice was what they need.
Once that very painful hour passed,
They were distributed in a mass.
Children confused, the older in a muse,
But no one was brave enough to start a fuse.
The man in command, had a whip in his hand,
Screamed that if they did not follow his commands.
They would be reprimanded, but no one could stand it,
Stories of pain, written on their sequoia skin, not even treated to bandages.
The blue sky made their skin cry tears of perspiration,
Nobody could understand the administration of this horrid nation,
One day Abraham Lincoln came along, said, "This is all wrong!"
While some were lucky enough to escape, many were left raw.
Refusal of the dictation, my skin color doesn't define my patriotism,
Black, brown, white, we're all the same organism.
Your laws try to protect me but I'm still left in the dirt,
But many people don't know how much freedom's worth.

Outside
by Timothy Blankenship

Outside bunnies hop
Outside birds chirp very loudly
Outside it is calm

Heaven Above
by Olivia Shelton

I've heard Heaven is a wonderful place
With fluffy clouds and the golden gate
The one who protected you, you will soon meet
The stairway to Heaven is the place to be
The angels with halos and shimmering wings
Who were looking after you and me
Singing high in the sky, oh how sweet
With love and care so heavenly
Meeting with my family once again
Arms open wide, a big smile on my face
I felt warm inside
And that's when I knew I was safe in this place
I know Heaven is a wonderful place
I will await for my time
It's filled with love to hold, and love to give
Heaven is above

Zeus, Come Home
by Savannah Harris

You left so soon
It will never be clear
It's almost noon
And you're not here
Where are you
I miss you
You were my fuel to my heart
You and me were like glue
Always there for me
On the beach and in my car seat
But you are now set free
You would always lick my cheek
Someday I will see you again
Can't wait for that day
You're always on my brain
When I see you, we will play again

Nature
by Joey McDermott

Big Brown Bear
With Enormous Brown Paws
Swipes At The Terrified Deer

There Was a Valley
by Kaitlyn Bakker

There was a valley where creatures roamed
They lived in peace, it was their home
The sun would rise, the sun would fall
Winter came and it would fall
The moose lived in peace
And the dogs ruled the land
The eagles flew in the sky
The hatchlings tried to fly
It was a beautiful place
Along came big yellow machines
They were cruel and mean
They burned the land
They turned the land
Into ash and dust, the rabbits were gone
The moose weren't around for long
Nature wasn't strong, there is no song

Storm
by Matthew Mainwold

I look out the window to see wind going wild outside
blowing trees around and around
making them lean towards one side until it stops and goes back.
The rumble of the storm makes me alerted and spooked
as trees move back and forth
just as my hand moves back and forth along the paper.
I remember times the wind has opposed me and it was scary days.
Ones that shook trees, and threw branches
and ones that pushed me back and forth.
As I stood my ground I leaned like I was synced
with the leaning trees, that also oppose the wind.
They go forth into battle for stability.
It feels like it will never back off, Mother Nature even fights herself.
The resistance does not give up as the tree shall still stand.
Hurricanes, tornadoes, earthquakes and the tree leans back and forth.
And, the tree still stands.

Summer
by Joey Myers II

Birds sing in the blue sky,
Green grass glistens in bright sun,
The soft wind whistled.

The End
by Taylor Wilson

Tick-tock
I hear the Reaper's song
The end knocks
Please let life get long
Reaper's scythe just in sight
Death's door opens up
The world goes white
As I drink from the devil's cup
Shadow creeps up on me
Chains tether me to the wall
Souls glide through black sea
Something begins to crawl
Minutes shave off
Life slips away
Let me skip the drop-off
Life extend I pray

The Fishing Trip
by Joshua Lepp

Vroom!
A moving boat
With me, Johnny, and Marissa sitting in the front,
The adults, my grandfather and uncle, are controlling it.
The wind flowing through my hair as we move,
Splash!
The sound of a bass jumping out of the water.
We start casting our rods,
Nothing, the word echoes in my head,
"I got something," Johnny says.
We all rush there to see what it is.
A branch.
We put it back in the water.
We get out of the boat and head back home.
We get Sonic because of thirst.
That memory will stay with me forever.

Defying Gravity
by Samantha Emler

Flowers grow toward
the sky. Despite gravity's
pulls to keep it down.

Ode To Nachos
by Joe Scaldo

Oh, nachos!
I can't live without thee!
Your taste is incomparable.
It makes me want to sing.
Your salsa like a fiery explosion!
Your cheese like melted wonder.
Whenever I eat you.
I never seem to ponder.
Whenever I feel cravings.
There's always one food I go to.
That of course is you, nachos.
My life revolves around you.
Oh, nachos!
Thy taste divine.
And that is why I am always thankful.
That you are always mine.

Where Am I?
by Molly Soukup

In a cloudless sky of discord,
The memories mourn.
And slowly,
Time withers away the hate and the hurt
But inside, I am empty.
The ground beneath me is crumbling away
But I have to keep going anyways
I wear a mask over my destroyed face,
And pretend to be as bright as sunshine
But really, I'm wandering through space.
Not knowing my next move,
Not knowing where to go
As if I am swimming in ebony water.
Like a lost child,
Not knowing my place in the world.
I am just another link in the chain.

The Great Siberian Tiger
by Summer-Sayra Johnson

The great big tiger
has big black stripes, black tipped tail
paws on the moist grass.

Years
by Morgan Franklin

The year started not long ago.
And so far there's been lots of snow.
Last year was great I have to say.
And I didn't want it to go.
St. Patrick's day is on its way.
It will be here in just a day.
Easter will be here super soon.
And when it's here there'll be bouquets.
Easter is here and plants will bloom.
There won't be any room for gloom.
Fourth of July is almost here,
Then we'll be back in the classroom
It will be the awesome new year
That is when people start to cheer.
The world spins too fast to slow down.
So you should live with zero fear.

Stages
by Brittany Montoya

New life awakens bees and birds,
The thought of new words are heard.
The birds in the trees fly high,
The flowers scattered like in a herd.
Sand, and sun shimmer in the sky.
Waves ruffling by as birds fly.
The smell of the salty ocean breeze,
The sun gone now, time to say bye.
The smell of flowers and the bees,
The pollen in the air, I sneeze.
Leaves on the ground like paper blow,
The trees' leaves are like a fresh breeze.
In the winter it is cold, snow,
Oh, don't you know it is known, though.
All trees are old and must all die,
Winter has come at last unknown.

Thunderstorms
by Chloe Dillon

Thunderstorms are sad
Thunderstorms are wet and cold
Thunderstorms have wind

A Beachy Day
by Hannah Farley

I have much fun beside the bay,
And this is where I want to stay.
It's where most people like to go,
Because they do not have to pay.
I love to feel the cold breeze blow,
And feel the sand beneath my toe.
I slowly smell the salty air,
And listen to the water flow.
I need sunglasses for the glare,
For the sun shines bright in my hair.
I know I have to soon say bye,
So now I'll pack my toys and chair.
I'm very tired in bed I lie,
Everyone around starts to cry.
My vision slowly starts to fade,
I look around and wonder why.

Hope
by Audrey Kelley

Everyone tells me not to worry
Everyone tells me not to stress
But they don't know my secret
That my emotions are a mess
No one has seen the things I've seen
Or knows the things I know
My emotions feed off my energy
Which causes my worry to grow
On days that are the worst
My head locks up, I cannot think
But there is only one thing
That can break the worry's link
When my head is pounding like a drum
And my eyes refuse to open
I see the smiling face of my friend
That I know I can put my hope in

Troubling Thunder
by Lauryn Field

The thunder is here.
Dark clouds and booms never leave.
Troubled times have come.

Dear People of the World
by Alivia Williams

I know you aren't perfect
I know you don't like yourself
But we both know,
You are worth it
You are beautiful
You can eat whatever you want
You should never be afraid to go to school
You should never be held down and felt low
You should never be anyone but yourself
Don't ever hang on your mistakes
You are loved, by me
Because you are only you,
And you know this yourself, too
We are all human
All different
And all are important

Thank You, Mother Nature
by Emalee Vickers

Oh, nature,
How much you are adored
You bring happiness and peace,
Hope and love
To all that is around.
Oh, nature,
You house the critters
That roam the floor at night.
You allow our trees to grow
From short and weak to tall and strong.
Oh, nature,
We thrive on you;
You provide warmth, shelter, and much more.
How much you are needed
Cannot be expressed.
Thank you, Mother Nature

Never Lost
by Audrey Zeren

I watch as my best friend
is laid down on the carpet
I bolt over to greet her
only to find her motionless
Motionless …
I gingerly touch her small, black furry head
I've known her my entire life
just to see her leave
My sweet Begheera,
Gone forever
Yet ... Never lost

No One
by Kendyl Nummy

No one sees me, they see a shell
No one knows me, they know a disguise
No one loves me, they love a fake
I want them to see, they would run
I want them to know, they would forget
I want them to love, they would hate
I'm tired of this shell they keep me in
I'm tired of this disguise they keep hidden
I'm tired of this fake, they keep me away
On Earth there's no escape
Keep hold of yourself every day

Therapy
by Brianna Martinez

The same green wall which was painted over because red was too violent.
The same couch that always dips in the same corner I sit in. Each time.
The same, "How are you doing this week?"
The same clicking pen and same sad eyes
as I share what has happened in my mind.
The same, "We're out of time,"
because these sessions only come once in a lifetime.
The same broken mind and hooded eyes.
The same, "Therapy isn't working for you, Brianna." What am I here for then?
The same, "Take these pills then hopefully you will get better.
Not now. But then."
When is then? When will then arrive? I hope I'm not dead before 'then'

Shall Never Be Enough
by Emerson Brenner

On a cold winter day;
All I can hear is the sway,
Not of the trees, not of the wind;
As I run the snow through my fingertips.
As I walk near the fire,
I can hear the flames;
Of the crackle of the wood;
Hitting the blaze.
As my hand lay near the fire;
I dream of flying higher;
With flowers of bloom,
And sun full of shine,
Stars full of light,
And a heart that is purely mine.
Then I lay my finger,
On the frosted grass;
With the numb of the clarity;
And love of the tough sun;
The love I hold for nature;
Shall never be enough.

Action
by Reagan Stierwalt

Ripples of history are shown to the beholder,
but ignorance shrouds the full truth.
The patterns in the tide, clear as summer rain.
Mistakes have been made, but instead of learning from our past,
we look in the future, when all of this has been lost in the back of our heads.
Old news flying by, but the truth is,
if we don't take action no one will have the motivation to.
You can say you'll do something,
but saying and doing are two separate people.
If you don't start no one will follow.
Segregate the wrong from right, our eyes see everything black and white
because we don't want to know.
We don't want to realize the world of grey we live in.
Yes some are darker shades,
but that doesn't mean we ridicule what we don't think is normal.
Our world is full of tides, crashing disasters and fun little waves.
Even the smallest wave can hurt.
And even the biggest crash can help.
Ripples of history is shown to you, don't let ignorance shroud your truth.

Play Again
by Leigha Vanorsdol

The calluses on my hands
Are worth far more than gold
The songs that have reverberated through this wood
Will forever keep their hold
On my heart and in my mind
The chords stretching my fingers down the frets
Though my fingertips do not feel like silk
I will never look at my Taylor with regret
The strings bent with the blues
And vibrated with acoustic rock
The voice of country
Flowing through the air as I strum with thought
The stories this guitar has told
The sorrows it has hummed
Just to bring back a happy tale
I sing my heart out
And bleed the tunes
I play till my fingers hurt
And then play again till they feel no more

Sunday
by Sophie Berry

Sitting in the car on the way home.
I felt the cool refreshing wind in my hair,
life was good but I did not know what lies ahead.
I got out of the car with my husband and grandchild,
my other daughter stayed home while we went to church.
The other daughter was sick but always seems fine
but today she was very sick.
She took her medicine like always, but this time she was weak and tired
she was sitting outside on the back porch.
Feeling like she needed fresh air, with the warm bright sun hitting her face.
She took her medicine, then fell asleep.
We arrived home, I opened the door and put my grandchild down for a nap.
My husband went to go change out of his church clothes
and I went to see how my daughter is.
I saw that my daughter was on the back porch.
I smiled at the sight of my sleeping daughter.
I opened the back door and I touched my beautiful daughter's face
to wake her up, hearing no response I touched her again.
She still did not move, dead, she was dead

Rain Drips
by Olivia Kailey

Rain Drips,
shadows fade, time stops, love ends, lines curve,
the panes of your window soaked from the outside.
So you turn to Truth.
Truth the color in a world so black.
Truth, the love in a hated world.
Truth the name you call for help.
Light darkens, noise drowns
hands meet, love's energy shared
life continues.
Rain Drips.

Grind
by Milan Thomas

You keep on going
Traveling the world to inspire.
When they ask you to jump,
You say how much higher.
Dream until your dreams aren't dreams anymore.
It's something you are reaching for.
You keep that fire and that desire.
Do it like it's your last
Because you will know you had a blast.
When it's time to go and you hear that chime
You will know that you left a great legacy behind.

Heat
by William Scoville

Walking in the desert with a camel, it was scorching hot-
we were baking like tater tots.
As we were walking, we saw a flower;
the flower had some type of power
of peace and love.
As I touched the flower, I had the power and tried to spread
as much as I could.
People would laugh, people would cry.
Whenever I came by, people would say bye,
until one day someone said hi.
I looked up and I saw an image of the one thing that made me work ... heat.

Ed Sheeran
by Chloe Provenza

Eraser
Dive

Shape of You
Happier
End Game
Everything Has Changed
Runaway
A Team
Nancy Mulligan

Sonnet For My Old Backyard
New York Memories
by Aidan Johnson

The endless woods of my old home stretch on.
A young explorer's grandest dream.
Through the sky of golden dawn.
Though childish it may seem.
Tallest trees imaginable, reach their wooden fingers to the sky.
Leaves, such beauties, as far as the eye can see.
So perfect, nature is, where nothing goes awry.
My father's hand-built swing set meant so much to me.
My thoughts linger to those glorious rides,
Where my dad would drive through the woods with me.
His familiarity with nature, our guide.
I can't help but remember my name carved in that tree.
Dawn moves on to dusk, and the days fade away.
Like the memories I hold from those childhood days.

Livvy
by Daelen Hammer

I begin to read so anxious to finish the last chapter
tick, tock, tick, tock the golden clock is chiming in my bedroom
The yellow of the pages is blinding my eyes, how can I go on?
She whips Cortana down
Crash!!! The sword breaks but then ...
It pierces through Livvy's heart
He runs to her
And I watch the sadness seep into his face
His baby, his baby girl, his Livvy is gone
And the golden clock chimes, the hour midnight
-In tribute to the ongoing Shadow Hunter series,
The Dark Artifacts: Lord of Shadows

Everything Everywhere
by Lilly Harris

In the misty morning air the trees sway
As the wind whispers them awake
In the hot gruesome afternoon the weeping willows weep
as their roots begin to wither
In the deep canyon the rock watches
as the wind howls out in pain
At the ocean's edge the fire roared with fury
for it could not harm the water
In the dark of night the rain seems to chase me
like an angry moose
Hidden under a roof the rain beats on top
angry that it cannot enter
At the break of dawn the sun is reborn
but dies again at dusk
The moon claws for the sky in the darkest of hours
and claws back down at light
During the dark and after the light nothing comes and everything goes
and the life drains away

The Lone Owl Calls
by Sarah Rahmatullah

The lone owl is calling, from its perch in the twisted tree.
The soft who-woo sounds again, a mournful, yet beguiling plea.
Who is the owl calling to, in his sorrowful tones?
To whom is this haunting strain directed to, from just outside his home?
The moon is full and radiant, its face knowing, soft, and plain.
She streams her shining, silvery rays to pool and drip below like shimmering rain.
A frosted river of sparkling stars adorn the sky's silky, inky tresses.
Soft, dark shadows drape themselves at the bases of trees, rocks, shrubs,
And the mouths of dark recesses.
What is the owl yearning for, on this stillest, most serene of nights?
Is that sorrow gleaming in his round yellow eyes,
Or are they just reflecting moonlight?
The river rushes through the shaded woods, a flow of liquid shadows.
The moonshine is reflected on it in writhing ribbons, gleaming flashes,
And floating specks.
Still the owl sits and broods on his stout tree branch.
His feathered chest rises and falls slightly with each wheezing breath.
What the owl longs for, we may never know.
All I can say is that he is lucky, to have made these enchanted woods his home.

My Dog
by Taylor Nixon

There was a tiny puppy
So sweet and cuddly
She was very playful
She was also very faithful
Her name was Baylee
Everyone thought it was Haylee
My dad got her when she was 6 weeks old
Mom was just told
She was stubborn
She would squirm and worm
She wouldn't sit still
She wouldn't just chill
She took care of my brother and sister
She never had the jitters
She ran away a couple of times
Everyone knew she was mine
One night her eye was irritated
But she wasn't frustrated
Dad took her to the vet
On 8-1-13 she was put down, she was the best pet

The Still Ocean
by Dani Marie Wright

Tan little grains on my bare feet
Soft but rough all at once
The colorful, multi shaped shells buried here
Many little creatures under there
Some small, some large, some in the clear
The soft fluffy foam washing on the shore
The sweet scent of summer air
Sitting in my wooden umbrella chair
Shades over my eyes to block the afternoon sun
A beach ball by my side for fun
The calming sound of waves, oh so soft
Surrounds me
Surfers all around me
Doing twists and turns in the waves
While I relax in the sun
The day is almost over
The sun's going down
It's getting quiet
It's time to go home
It's time for the ocean to be still

3rd Place

Sarah Taylor

Just Another Inconvenience
by Sarah Taylor

All of us rushing on the worn lanes of concrete and asphalt
Built by the hands of workers long-forgotten
Gazing through the pane of glass that separates me from them
Wondering if they, too, were headed home
Saying an inaudible prayer
that we would reach our destinations without harm
Streetlamps illuminated our passages of stone
But looking up into the deep shadow of night, I found no light
The glare of the city as impressive as it is
Should bow to the infinite brilliancy of stars
Yet, somehow they were gone
Cloaked by the synthetic light of man
The ghost of a tear formed in my eyes
For the loss of the hidden beauty
A little farther down trail at the corner of my vision
Rested a hint of greenery protruding from a fault in a sidewalk
It's a funny thing, isn't it?
This unwanted bit of green rising above the pathway
That was meant to eliminate such inconveniences
For easy walking.

2nd Place

Alessandra Brown

The Promised Land
by Alessandra Brown

I have seen the promised land,
Where black and white walk hand in hand.
Equal in the eyes of the Lord
Yet the whip still lashes, drawing innocent blood
The slave woman hears her child wail,
torn away like a calf to slaughter
Scarred backs bent under the scorching sun
Callused feet throb and ache,
Rough hands grasp at fronds of wheat
Tearing stalks with arthritic joints
The slave boy sits by a dying candle
which weeps tears of pearly wax
He slowly traces letters with slender brown fingers
Across the Holy Bible's faded verse
Above, the dove soars, abiding no command
Alight on the golden wings of freedom
Northward
Towards the promised land.

Alex Beynon

Biographical information not provided

The Ballad of Her
by Alex Beynon

I watched as she spun around on the tips of her toes
Rain cascading around her.
A graceful arch surrounding a graceful pirouette
Her arms outstretched
And face towards the heavens
In intoxicating bliss.
Her bright eyes,
And brighter smile,
All made her more beautiful
Than the rose in her hair.
The small laugh that escaped red-stained lips,
Her long dark hair that flowed elegantly,
And the feeling in my stomach
When she turned to me
And whispered,
"Dance with me"
All told me what I already knew.
That nothing
Would bring me more joy
Than her own.

Division III

Grades 8-9

Clock
by Anna Cates

As I wait, I long for your presence
I crave you being here, I crave your essence
Time is long without you, the nights are cold as well,
But as the clock ticks, I wish you well

Teens In 2018
by Emma McClure

Being a teen in 2018 is crazy.
It feels like yesterday we were all just a baby.
There's drama starters and cruel people.
We start drama on social media.
Which ends out in fights,
Or just causes suicide ...
There's ones who do drugs,
They don't care if they get a bug!
Being a teen can be fun ...
But we're all so, very dumb.

Sweet Juliet
by Melody David

Oh Juliet, sweet Juliet.
You died for a man you had just met.
Life made it clear that your love should have never been.
Yet you loved, and married, and now your life is at an end.
You gave this man a ring.
Because in your eyes he was a king.
The two families had hatred between each other.
It caused one from each house to die, both lovers
And the war between both families stopped.
Only because the two star-crossed lovers had dropped.

Mysteries, Puzzles, and Books
by Chandler Frisina

Mysteries, puzzles, and books
A way for me to relax and let things go
They make me feel like I am watching a show
The rush, the hook of a good mystery book
At the end of the day while others often play
When I sit down with a puzzle or book
The world and my worries just drift away
Oh how I wish I could stay in my reverie every day
But alas reality calls me back without delay
This is how I cope with life day by day

Student Athlete
by Tyler Strain

She on me
She on me
gotta get these grades
so I don't have to feel Mama's rage
I do my best to carry it all
but without my education
I could lose it all

The Precious Flower
by Kylie Bauer

We keep getting poked by the same thorn,
but still only see the beauty of the rose.
We are captivated by the lust,
we are drawn to the deep red,
that disguises the painful prick.
The flowering of hope,
and the inspiration to grow.
We continue to crave
the beauty of the precious flower.

Living Your Own Life
by Kamilya Lyons

Life is a journey that goes on and on
You grow, succeed and learn new things
With people around, what joy that brings
You look at nature and its lovely colors
The grass, the sky and lots of others
Flowers in the ground growing here and there
While butterflies and other insects fly in the air
Life is like an ocean, constantly flowing
So live your best life so you can be constantly growing

Terrible Day
by Gabriel Griffin

When I heard the bell, I started to see Hell
They say to have fun but all I can hear is run!
I can see the others' doom but all I can do is run to the room
It's like rolling the dice to see if I suffice
My friend got impaled by a nail
But when it was over, I thought I was a lucky clover
Lucky for me I didn't die but I did cry
When I saw my dad, I was so glad
It was so terrible but somehow bearable

Will You Marry Me?
by Weslee Shear

Oh, you ensnare me with your loving glare
And you grow a garden of hope and care,
While I still care what I decide to wear.
And you talk to me and give me a dare,
But I cannot pull myself to love purely.
You will love me the same way forever.
And we gaze into each other with an endearing stare,
and our love never changes anywhere ever.
So I close my eyes and love you tonight
As if I was on my last day with you
And it sickens me with an unending blight
To believe you love me as I love you
And if our love is a never-ending story,
I don't want this one question pending ...

Blue Eyes
by Morgan Boesel

I lie between these burning sheets, between your hands
Are you even here? A dream again
I believe it's better named an obsession
My hand through your hair, as your alabaster skin sears into mine
If this is pain, then dear God, what do people call pleasure,
because I could lie in your heat all day
That one time we held hands, you set me alight
My face, my fingers, my heart
You burned my fingerprints away,
but why would I need them when I have the scars you left on me
My fingerprints are gone now, but I don't need them, I needed you
If eyes are the window to the soul, then your soul must be full of knives,
for nothing has ever pierced me like your stare
Dear God, when I am with you I am in Heaven, but Heaven says you're a sin
Does that make you Hell?
If you are the fires of Hell, come to take me, then please, do as you wish
My blue eyed demon, when they described demons,
they didn't say how addictive they are
When they described demons, I did not envision a chiseled face
like that of an angel, but angels don't sear into skin
The gates of Heaven are a mile from me, maybe less,
but a long walk when I hear you calling my name
from behind the gates of Hell, that press into my scorched back
My blue eyed demon,
when they described demons, I did not think I could love one
Your alabaster skin, with moonlight dancing upon it, take me, incinerate me,
I am yours, my blue eyed demon
Perhaps I should not love the feeling of your flames on my skin,
but how can I resist, when all I see is Blue?

One Demand
by Dusty Whiddon

My heart is a park.
For all my friends
To put their marks.
While we hold hands.
Peace is our drum.
And we only have one demand.
Don't fight a war with guns.
Play the pin in your hands.
And come to an agreement.
So we can all live together.
This is to be meant.
So we can live forever.
In the knowledge
Of our successors.
To follow our lineage.

The Struggle
by Abdiel Caraballo

What is the struggle of a man,
Is he fearful of his own pride, or is he fearful of his ego,
Is he scared of any authority, are there any bounds of what the man can't do?
But in true light, when the sun fades away
and the pride swells back to an empty hollow spot in his soul,
and strength only carries through the day,
at night the man does struggle.
Is the struggle of the man his humanity, his emotion?
When that pride and ego go away, the emotions peek their ugly grin,
Because in a society where happiness is the key for success,
luxurious life, and a happy ending.
Because in the end we ask, "What is the struggle?"
Is it right to repress this cocktail of emotion.
Or is the struggle of a man the popularity around him,
All the people around him trying to become famous
by ridiculing and making fun of serious things, is this right?
But with all of this, and the struggle of not being popular or happy
Does not even compare to the death, destruction, and misery
that people are passing in other places.
How can a society say, "We are more connected than ever before."
But the real struggle is that we can't even as a society bring us closer
by a "Hello" or "How are you?"
But the struggle of a man is being discriminated for being human.
The emotions we feel are a part of us and instead of acknowledging it
we push it away like an outcast.
When did "your cancer" or "I'm gonna kill myself" become a game
and not a more serious topic.
When this became the struggle of a man ...

When You Left
by Amanda Kelce

I know now it's too late
It shouldn't have to end this way
You were supposed to be my soulmate
I feel like I'm in a crate
You made my days not feel so gray
I know now it's too late
Now I sit in my room and blat
Here me out, I have more to say
You were supposed to be my soulmate
I thought we were brought together by fate
I have cried out all my tears and I feel like dried-up clay
I know now it's too late
My burdens feel like a weight
You were the one who always led the way
You were supposed to be my soulmate
I should have been the one who cleansed the slate
I want you to stay
I know now it's too late
You were supposed to be my soulmate

The Four Seasons
by Zoë Sampson

The comforting pitter-patter of the rain falling from the sky
covers the new blooms of spring as they grow;
emanating their gentle, sweet aroma.
New life coming to our world, all the while the sun peeks from the leaves
who create a canopy of protection.
The fresh green grass underneath our feet awakens as water from a waterfall
flows gently, calmly down into a pond, where fish swim and thrive
and deer stop to rest and gaze upon the calm hot day.
The birds take rest in the trees as a gentle warm wind blows,
singing its song in sequence with the birds and the leaves.
The leaves slowly, gently, falling from slumbering giants like doves flying down
where the birds leave and the deer stay and as it gets colder
it gets calmer, such as a bear about to sleep.
The frost encases plants like a blanket
and snow sparkles like diamonds, a white soft powder.
Icicles cling to rooftops like a bat would to a cave,
cold beauty as Mother Nature creates a blanket of frost leaving her art
in the swirls of frost almost creating a still dance.
The four seasons come together, each with their own beauty and elements.
Spring brings forth life to our world and nurtures it.
Summer lets fun and freedom into new life.
Fall calms and allows rest and healing
And winter brings beauty and elegance with its own art and calmness
that allows growth within a blanket of white protection.

New Beginnings
by Denae Johnson

A young girl sits in the back of the class,
Quiet as death,
Her lips set in a grim line,
A vacant look in her eyes.
The room is in chaos around her
But she stays still,
Like a statue frozen in time
And dreams about a time before.
When a vicissitude has not yet torn her life apart,
And a wide smile crinkled her shining eyes
a golden-haired girl standing beside her.
Their laughter ringing through the air like bells,
Funeral bells, she realizes now,
To mark the end of a dying friendship.
But a comforting hand is placed on her shoulder,
And she snaps back to the present.
A promise fresh in her mind,
She won't dwell in the past, any longer,
But will focus on the new beginnings before her

Like No One Else
by Emma Hibberd

I've never felt these things before.
When we sit close, I barely breathe. You knew that, didn't you?
When I'm next to you, I feel in the slightest, limitless.
I usually feel powerless in this cruel world.
But not with you. Sometimes it's like no one else is there.
Just you and me. You seem to understand me like no one else does.
Everyone thinks there is something wrong with me.
People think the same of you too, I guess.
We're not so different. Yet, we're opposites.
You seem confused when I stare as you laugh. How could I not?
It's unexplainable really, I guess I like seeing you happy.
I know I hate it when you are down on yourself.
You're beautiful in your own way.
You're like shattered stained glass. Bright and colorful, yet sharp.
I will pick up your pieces until my hands bleed.
I will mend your broken wings and straighten your bent halo.
You're worth it.
Do I silence the voices in your head? Do I numb some of the pain?
When you're with me, do you feel okay? Do you feel wanted?
Do you feel loved? Do you feel safe?
All of these occur when I'm with you.
I don't know how you do it. I don't know why it happens.
I don't understand you fully. But I want to.
I want to understand you like you understand me. Like no one else does.

Seasons
by Ethan Gilmore

Spring is a fun time
Winter is very chilly
Fall is fantastic

Love
by Morgan Barnes

I love you today
As I have from the start
And I'll love you forever
With all of my heart
Once upon a time
I became yours
And you became mine
We will be together
Until the end of time
I wish you could see
The angel I see
When you stand
In front of me
Your eyes shine
Like a million stars
You shine more brightly
Than anyone

Friends
by Corinna Fittje

I am beautiful and strong
I wonder what real friends are
I hear my bed comforting me
I see people getting along
I want real friends
I am beautiful and strong
I pretend I have real friends
I feel fake friends all around me
I touch the Bible in search for real friends
I worry about the fake friends
I cry about the real friends drifting away
I am beautiful and strong
I understand not everyone is a real friend
I say Jesus is the answer to all your problems
I dream of a world with no fake people
I try and pray for all the fake people
I hope Jesus helps them realize what they are doing
I am beautiful and strong

How I See the World
by Alexandrea Forsell

In my sight
I see the world
In many ways
That are hard to explain.

Seventeen
by Aedan Evans

Seventeen, Seventeen killed
How the whole nation was chilled
Seventeen, Seventeen lines
For the people this poem enshrines
Seventeen, Seventeen lives
From the shooter's hate these victims derive
Seventeen, Seventeen we love
Seventeen we will always be proud of
Seventeen, Seventeen to remember
For our love for them is a burning ember
Seventeen, Seventeen faced a terrible downfall
Even though our boys in blue stood tall
Seventeen, Seventeen that were good
Most of which were still in childhood
One, One with hate in his heart
One, One that tore the world apart
- Dedicated to the Stoneman Douglas High School victims

Hidden Hearts
by Akasha Thorne

A splash of color,
Bright and full of light,
Contrasting with the darkness,
And the loneliness of night.
A soft hum of hope,
A melody of happiness,
Casting away the shadows,
The rules, the religious,
Joyful in their own,
But simply because they are happy;
This kind of happy can never be shown.
One pair of parents support and give joy,
In one house there is no joy, the child is the parent's toy,
In the other there may be hope, she has found a way to cope,
These children rest their heads on separate beds
But at school their hands are tightly wound
Their glare is a dare for society to tear them apart.

My Journey
by Garrett McClelland

I walked up to a tree and got stung by a bee
At the tree I saw a book and it was about hooks
After I left the tree I encountered smog
While walking through I saw a dog.
I saw a king get a ring,
I rode my bike and put a kite in the sky and flew it

The Big One
by Austin Simmons

Fields of green
Seas of blue
But you must be keen
or you'll surely lose
Fish on! Fish on!
as the skippers yelled on
with water splashing
the fish were thrashing
As we fought
the line became taut
closer and closer
the beast grew near
An ugly monster
is what we brought closer and closer
to which, this was the mistake
the greatest cost it would take

The Need For Speed
by Isaac Wadkowski

Racing is at the core of
A person that has the need for
Speed, then followed by hard
Work and to be relentless even if
Someone says quit, the need
For speed is something I
Live off, finally the need
For speed is where it starts off,
The thrill of being thrown
Back into your seat, the wind racing
By, the engine roaring like
A lion in your ears, the smell
of burnt rubber, the sweet
Smell of the fuel, the heart pounding
Out of your chest is
Something I don't ever want to forget.

A Great Woman
by Trynt Morkes

Her smile lights up the world
Her laugh is deep and quiet like a piano
Her kindness knows no bounds
Her voice is low and pleasant
Her eyes speak many words silently and hide brilliance
She is a great woman

The Flames
by David Papa

The flames could be dancers.
They bounce and jump around.
When they find their victims,
They're not graceful dancers any more.
They eat.
They engulf.
They destroy.
Until all that's left is the memory of the victim.
They move on with no remorse,
no recollection of what they did.
Then they go back to dancing,
they bounce and jump around.
Until the dancers get tired,
and start to lay down.
Then water makes them a blanket,
As the water is the new destroyer.

The Tomb of Fallen Foes
by Makayla Roy

Hark! Villain,
If thou darest enter this somber cave
let ye be warned
thou enters the Tomb of Fallen Foes
Upon these walls here writ
are the names of heroes long gone.
If ye finds favor with their spirits
Thou shalt be blessed with the power
of their living days, also their purpose.
In the furthermost chamber of this cave
lies a book bound in bloody leather
carved into its pages are the names
and spirits of horrid villains.
If ye enter with greed or lust for power
Ye may find thouest their slave and vessel.
Thou hath been warned.

Life On the Farm
by Meghan Shue

life on the farm has
nice red dirt as red
as crimson and tractors
that sit like a lump
a barn to park the trucks
and tools for the farmer

Summarized Romeo and Juliet
by Abigail McManus

Two star-crossed lovers
Came from feuding families
Which must recover
From the awful realities
That their beautiful Juliet
And their intelligent Romeo
Have been secretly wed
By Friar Lawrence- documented on folio.
Out of anger between the two houses
They lost members of each household,
But eventually make the right choices:
They finally get a hold
On the dreadful situation.
But it's too little, too late
After the collaboration
They find what they've created.

A Different Night
by Kailyn Milne

The sound of slamming doors and breaking glass
Was a sound she got used to very fast
The act of him leaving stayed the same
But every night she still felt the pain
He always left and always came back
That's why tonight she had a heart attack
That night, she felt as if she were dead
As ten thousand thoughts ran through her head
He was the first and last man she loved
She liked it better when he just gave her a shove
Now he was gone, gone forever
He would never come back, never ever
She was so hurt, she cried and cried
She missed all of his goofy ties
It might not seem like it would hurt that much
But she called him Daddy, that should explain enough

Basketball
by Michael Zdon

Hit the court when we hear the crowd roar,
Music blaring, eyes staring
The whistle blows, everyone flows
Here we go, game time, bro
We're on the court going back and forth
With the ball we always score, fourteen and zero, we're on a roll
We're on the loose, facing good teams and bad teams we never lose
We're on the road to glory, we never back down and that's my story.

She Flows
by Sarah Boodoo

Once every month
The river overflows
into the valley.
From within
Her flow
cannot be stopped
For it is the work
Of nature herself.
Yet they try to stop her
That flow in not of
What they need.
Yet they boast
Of all the quality
Her flow's fertility
Brings.

Home
by Kyliegh Dickerson

It surrounds me, every waking moment is a reminder of you.
It has consumed me. It has surrounded me. You.
I remember the days, the nights, the evenings, the fights.
We were close, I think we still are.
You are my friends, brother, teacher.
You taught me everything. I wish I would've been prepared,
When it was time for you to go Home.
Home may be different for you now.
For me, it's where you were.
You're not here anymore though, I don't know where I am.
I don't know what I'm doing.
Going through life like a doll.
Emotionless, heartless, fearless.
Doing everything I can, to keep everyone safe.
Not afraid if I go Home to meet you again.

Sisterhood
by Alexus Yale

Between us are a lot of secrets
most things unsaid
some things are frequent
some things are in my head
Sisters have a special bond
a special place in my heart
we will love each other beyond
nothing can split us apart

Sadness
by Billie Humphreys

i don't wanna die, i just wanna vanish for a while
truly i hate this life
and all the time
i cry
so many fiery tears
combining with my anxious fears
the anxiety rising up into my head
my hands are shaking, what am i gonna do
i can't message, i've already bothered you
it's so hard
being this far
from any type of happiness
and a way to cope, to be at bliss
i just want a solution
i don't think i can handle this

Melancholy Girl
by Marissa Miley

Melancholy girl
I wonder where it all went wrong
I hear the past, I see time fly
I want to be something
Melancholy girl
I pretend to be okay
I feel empty, I touch fading scars
I worry about the future
I cry at your words
Melancholy girl
I understand it eventually gets better
I say everyone deserves to live a happy life, but can't find one for myself
I dream for a better tomorrow
I hope you stay
Melancholy girl

broken
by Danielle Ayres

A love so strong, so true, they said I do
As the years passed
their love did not last
Another caught his eye
so he said goodbye
Now she is here
picking up the pieces
of her broken heart

Waves of Society
by Carlie Vestle

Waves crash down; society tumbles on top of me.
"Follow your heart," they say.
I have the weight of the world on my shoulders.
Waves start coming in harder and more fiercely.
I am hit with pressure
pressuring me to be a certain way and act a certain way.
The pressure gets the best of me.
I lose all hope
in who I want to become as a child in society.
Water starts to fill my lungs.
I could've stepped out before the waves became hectic.
Maybe the current would've pulled me back.
The waves take over.
I am too busy trying to be perfect.
I have finally lost touch of the real me.

Insanity
by Catherine Keene

As sanity escapes my grasp
I cannot find my heart and mind
my mind, my mind
My mind is a stranger to me now
I grope in the darkness of my heart
searching for something
something, something
Something to know and grasp and love
Just a memory will suffice
Anything but the dreams
dreams, dreams
The dreams my mind makes me see
Anything but the screams
screams, screams
The screams my mind makes me hear

Smile More, Eat Less
by Hailey Free

Society screams smile more, eat less
Society is the fuel to this generation's stress
The same one that shames girls in a size five dress
The same one all of these girls they try to impress
Society will continue to scream smile more, eat less
Until we all fit in that size zero dress
And your life is consumed in all of the stress
Until your stomach stops growling I'm hungry
And starts screaming good job.

Tick, Tick, Tick
by Kaeleigh Sudary

Don't be afraid of clocks
Tick, tick, tick ...
Time has been extremely generous to us
Time has been very precious to us
We've done nothing– nothing– but waste time on useless stuff
We have conquered faith at a certain time
And at a certain place
Tick, tick, tick ...
Time has given us the taste of sweet victory
Time has given us the taste of loss and sadness
Tick, tick, tick ...
We have so much time but instead
We waste it
Tick, tick ...
Tick.

Romeo and Juliet
by Brielle Yoder

A pair of young lovers, star-crossed by fate,
Were derived from two families overcome with hate.
Though both sought freedom, peace, and life,
Despite all their actions came the killer: strife.
But in the midst of all the chaos, the light of their love grew.
They were safely hidden by the night, when nightingales flew.
But why, O joy, must you be choked by pain?
Quarrels turn to death, where blood has lain.
Steal, rob, and kill the last hopeful rays.
Exile love and sink beneath tragedy's waves.
Separation will cause another to seek her ring.
If all is lost, a powerful knife can take the sting.
And if every plan fails, the result will be death,
For if one lover passes ... the other must take his own breath.

Catch Me If You Can
by Alyssa Raley

Catch me if you can,
You can try but you will fail,
As we streak across the field,
Catch me if you can,
I yell as we thunder past the prancing deer,
Me and my steed flying, soaring,
Racing the wind, the gods above,
Catch me if you can,
But you won't,
For we are in the stars.

The Writing of a Poem
by Thomas Smith

I see the white striped paper
It's staring me in the face
I have an objective
Due at a time and place
The thing I can't figure out
Is what to write about?
Should I write a about the cold?
Or someone really old?
Should it be scary?
Or about some kind of berry?
Should it show shopping shoppers?
Or all the grasshoppers?
The one thing that I know
Is that it's due tomorrow!

Freakshow
by Skye Rustad

The honk-ity-honk from the clown's red nose
The dripping face paint falling down their face
The squirts of water from the flower hose
The clowns chasing the kids like it's a race
The freaks come alive at the break of night
When the kid-friendly creatures go to sleep
They run to the hills and follow the light
Which tells them dinner is ready to eat
Their teeth are sharp enough to take an arm
Watch out 'cause they could be under your bed
Their eyes are black and cause just as much harm
Their death is brought by a shot to the head
When they are gone their stories will live on
And their spirits will haunt from beyond

Ring the Bell
by Camden Friend

Our gloves are on
We turn from friends to foe
For twelve three-minute rounds
We are all go
We tell the refs let's go
For which we are ready to rumble
When they ring the bell, six rounds to go
On with no one to stumble
Round twelve to come, I get energized
He's on the mat by which I realized
I've knocked him out 9 ... 10 ... I win

Fragments of the Unwanted
by Lillianna Van Gemert

The more I read; the more I begun to understand the world around me.
To see the isolation of colors,
the fragments of the unwanted clouds wandering,
Though, as I go from word upon chapter
of shaking connections and choking beliefs.
I begin my world of lies, a web that is a placement- a graveyard for my words
My trust, my very being within this web of unwantedness.
To hear my own cries from a cage, trapped and unsure.
Where would a key be- beyond my reach.
Soaring and swaying above the ground in wonder and curiosity
plague my mind, feelings awake and alive till they drown and smoke
in the scorching fires that rage across my eyes.
Smiling, laughing and breathing feel fake;
walking on cold thin ice that curls and cracks on the greeting darkness-
Stars stretch beyond the reach of our hands,
intertwining with the lines and sketches of our fears.
Burning calls that blaze upon my ears, and the cold embrace of realization-
I'm searching for an escape, a way to spread my wings
and to not be tied down by the past spreading or the dreams howling.
To hear, to see, and to speak as one is deafening one's song.
For the conclusion, that paints the wall's identity-
the garden grew weak and ugly.
Flowers dim and lights wilt as the caressing thoughts
graze and bury in the soil that decorate the house
Of my mind, echoing and clawing at the walls of my confinement.
Isolation, loneliness, detachment, aloofness, hiding ...
are a few words that describe what I may feel on the skin of my body.
The itch and scratch of pain that surrounds me in a box
Of what is left of my imagination-
illusions and tricks of what is moral and immoral upon one's mind.
The more I read; the more I begun to understand the world around me.
To see the isolation of colors, the fragments of the unwanted.

F451
by Hunter Crawford

Guy Montag was his name
Starting fires was his game
Books engulfed by flames
Never to be the same
One day he meets Clarisse
She makes his mind cease
She was being watched by the police
May she now rest in peace
Montag reads a book
Which he had took
His wife is shook
So she calls him in as a crook
As his house is being ransacked
He figures out his captain is a maniac
So Montag fights back
Captain Beatty is killed in the attack
After this display
Everybody thinks he is insane
In the city he can no longer remain
He is forced to run away
- Inspired by the novel "Fahrenheit 451" by Ray Bradbury

Pounding Headaches of Sadness
by Isabel Almengor

Darkness ... a meaningful color our bodies contain.
It's trapped in such a timeless sense.
The feelings in my headaches complain and from the pain of my body's defense.
Push aside the dust of trapped feelings and nothing to wonder, nothing to care.
Alone in a chair, others eating– they are happy.
Still no feeling brought upon the quiet.
As I thought to myself, another headache.
More screaming, I'm still to fight it.
Shadows taking over– roaming, I am in despair.
Invisibility, a film over my body, no one there.
Another headache, not as bad, but not leaving.
I don't understand– happy people breathing.
No sadness– nowhere to be found. How is that in my body, it's all around?
One thing I do not know, for me, it isn't a choice.
How can I recover without a voice?
Eating is too painful, but to feel is painless.
To feel this way, for me it's effortless.
Tell me one thing; having a voice is important,
But choosing not to use it, is it the wrong choice?
My headaches are being accompanied with stomachaches, still nothing inside.
Yet now, the feelings in my body are choosing to die.

Missing Paws
by Ariana Moreno

After years of playing for hours and hours, I can no longer call you ours
Without you at my home, my mind was left to roam
Are you happy with your new owners? Mom and I feel like loners
I miss playing tag with you, when I was sad or mad you always knew
We would go outside by the field, and watch the sunset with our eyes peeled
I had cried when you left, I told myself it was for the best
Every night you would whine and whine, until finally I would say fine
Pick you up and put you on my bed, close your eyes and rest your head
You will always be in my heart, no matter how far apart
My worst day in a poem, without you I am no one.

o' thy lost inside own mind
by Melissa Allen

If there is one you are searching for,
something that would make life a breeze,
that you can't live without,
then you need to find it.
Know it may be the hardest thing to find.
When you think you have found it,
be careful not to let it go easy.
Once it is found you must promise to never let it go.
Hold on as long as you can.
Know when you have found it &
never forget how it feels to have it.
For once you give it away you will want to know how good it was to have.
It will be even harder to get it back than it was to get in the first place.
So do yourself a favor and never, I mean, never let go.

Into the Books
by Robert Picardo, Jr.

There in the library is a man with a passion.
He to the books is like a diva to fashion.
He read and he read to forget all his sorrow
Until, to no avail, it would come back tomorrow.
"Why, oh, why must the world be so?
Why can't it be back to the way it was long ago?"
He wept and he cried for hours on end
For the stories of the past which the librarians would lend.
Into the newspaper, all he would see,
Would be drugs, rape, shootings, arguments, and bent knees.
"Is this really all the world has to show?
There must be something happy that the people would like to know!
If there is nothing in here, then I guess it must be so.
Back into the books I go."

Back In the Fall
by Rachael Higgins

Back in the fall
I put up a wall
So I saw what people did
The broken glass forced to break free
Back in the fall

The Rose
by Kaelyn Rowan Lawrence

"the rose rebelled
until her thorns came in
now they rip and scar
from under her skin."
she wished she could go back
remembering her innocence past
too soon her soul turned black
and she was gone with a single blast
the rose is gone
now he is alone
now he feels like he has no home
because of the rose
she couldn't go back
but she watched him from above
she knew he wanted her back
"i'm so sorry, my love."

Depressed (Her Last Words)
by Tori Coburn

Just an average girl
She always wore a smile
She was cheerful and happy for a short while
Now she's older
Things are getting colder
Life's not what she thought, she wished someone had told her
Tried to stop herself from crying almost every night
But she knew there was no chance of feeling alright
Summer came by, all she wore was long sleeves
'Cause those cuts on her wrists were bleeding through you see.
She wrote a letter with her hand shaking wild
"Look at me now! Are you proud of your precious child?
I'm watching over you from the clouds above
And sending down the purest and whitest dove
To watch over you, and be my helpful eye
So this is it, world, goodbye."

Future Generations
by Saydea Southerlend

Can we as a nation
Try to avoid separation
By contemplating creation
And let positivity be a personal medication
And watch happiness come out of isolation
Only then could we be an inspiring demonstration
For our future generations

My Life
by Peyton Townsend

middle school crushes
stupid little fights
heartbeat rushes
always have to be right
watching my life as it forms
in 5 years I'll be in a college dorm
making new friends as I grow
I love everyone that I've grown to know
my lovely life is all my own

To My Future Husband
by Kara Davey

I know I have many faults
I know I'm hesitant to trust you
I know that you need me there
But one day I'll say, "I Do"
I'll smile as I walk down the aisle
I'll smile when I watch you play with our kids
I'll be there for you when you cry
I'll try to be the best and most supportive wife
For my future husband

The Disease
by Braedyn Main

I hate the disease
I would get on my knees
Only if someone would cure this disease
I would be pleased
I had a family member who used to rush around
But now all he can do is rush in my head
This disease is called cancer
I just wish we had all the answers
So Rush could just rush around

Motion of 1 and 2
by Parker McDaniels

Life's a motion
of 1 and 2,
you hit the ground
not knowing who,
then through life
with a groove,
to the end of life
that you approve.

The Dark
by Kya Sanders

It stays through the night,
It lurks in those who have had to fight.
The dark lingers in the past,
But will come back very fast.
It fights to consume more than just the light,
When it catches its next victim they might have a fright.
They forget everything good even their first kite
as they begin to be like the night and shut out the light.

The Forbidden Love
by Briana Cruz

give me a breath, give me some time
my heart aches as you say goodbye,
you gave me a chance and I did you wrong,
so you went to something suitable,
I want you to be happy and be a good man
don't get confused with a tramp,
just as charming and just as sweet
but will never give the love you need

God's Mercies
by Paige Ashley

God's freely given mercies, upon me, Jesus kissed
Are too numerous to list.
They are more infinite than the grains of sand that fill this earth,
And are angels' hands that pull me to my rebirth.
They dance throughout my life filling me with glee,
As the prodigal son's father danced, God's mercies do with me.
They show True Love at my worst and at my best;
Do I believe? It's a no question test!

Us
by Sydney Boswell

You say I'm young and childish
You say I haven't seen things
You, the adult, the naysayer
You who saw the towers fall
And who heard the King's words
You think we haven't seen our own horrors
You think we don't have our own heroes.
I say I'm strong and mature
I say I have my own nightmares
I, the future, the on-goer
I who was less than 200 miles from the Parkland shooting
I who heard Obama's words.
I have had to live knowing it could be me staring down the barrel
I also live knowing I could be a female president
We say we are hopeful and capable
We have seen things and know we will see more
We, the united, the present
We who don't jest, but take it in stride
We who will be our own heroes
We can do it on our own
But we want you to know we want you with us.

My Teenager Life
by Veronica Corado

It's hard to be a teenager no one really knows
What the pressure is in school
Well this is how it goes
I wake up every morning
And stare into this face
Every day it's just the same
I feel like a disgrace
Walking up into the world
It feels like it's just twirled
Homework here and homework there
I fall and I just swear
Teacher tells me, "Listen … you gotta do your work.
Stop wasting time, give it a try, and stop being a jerk."
My first love was a lie
He looked just like a fly
I walked, I laughed and pretty much died.
This teenager life
It's really hard
But the choices and the people
Use common sense.
It's tough being a teenager no one really knows.

The Lake House
by Spencer Brown

Getting up early in the morning
The taste of breakfast is never boring
Going outside after the rain
The smell will never bring me pain
Going on a mule ride after lunch
Hearing the gravel road crunch
The feeling of wet grass
And the handle made of brass
I love going on the boat and Jet Ski
Then seeing the flowers and the bees
And the animals I see
Under the giant oak tree
The eagles and the deer
I hear their sounds in my ears
Then we have hot dogs over the fire
After we start to feel tired
Then I wake up early in the morning
Then I know that surely
That today will beat yesterday
I can't wait to start the day!

Remember a Better Tomorrow
by Nathaniel Vilardo

Regrets, that's all I have left as I recall my misdeeds,
My life is a self-conjured mess, and now it's my time to clean,
I remember every excuse, every tight noose,
Every faint cry, never knowing why,
After every mistake and all the self-hate,
Yes, I remember everything,
I'm human, yet a machine, carrying my heavy clockwork heart,
While I stay up late praying, that somehow my life could restart,
I remember every excuse, every demon let loose,
Every cold tear and the undying fear,
All the self-harm that left scars on my arm,
Yes, I remember everything,
I was ruined, with a heart as black as coal as I tied more loops into the rope,
But all who have a pure soul saved me and gave me hope,
I remember every embrace, every kind face,
Every forgiving weep, as their love for me runs deep,
All who chose to forgive also chose to let me live,
Yes, I remember everything,
Hope, that's what repaired my being, my proof that miracles are real,
And no matter what you're feeling,
people are always there to hope and to heal.

Caring Protector
by Justin Farrell

Nature protects you
You like it as a friend
It is a family member
That cares for you
And helps you

I Don't Know What Grey Is
by Charlotte Grimes

I don't know what grey is
I don't just "kinda" feel things
The glass isn't half full
It's either full or empty
I can sleep forever
Or not sleep for three days
I can be stressed beyond belief
Or stable and take all the pain
I can eat a whole buffet
Or starve myself till I'm thin
I can push you away
Or I can let you in
I can love you with passion
I can hate you the same
Like I said in the beginning
I just don't see grey

The Clutch of Remorse
by David Puig

The grip of grass beneath my palms
To ensure the wind won't blow me far
For the storm of reality gave me qualms
The burden of the falling night was quite bizarre
I had looked upon the starlight gaze
That had left my heart to anticipate
I've sat upon these very grounds
From the moment memory began to pass
Although tonight was different
I had felt a single rolling tear
A tear of pain and remorse lifted off my cheeks
A tear conjured from deep within
For I was alone
Without home
Yet my spirit remained alive
At least until the day my memory passed by

Life
by Blake Paul

Life goes by too fast
For people to live in their past
We watch our lives go by
But no one questions why
Why commit a crime
All it does is waste your time
This doesn't mean make your life a race
Always keep a steady pace
If you always do your best
You will succeed like the rest
Plan your dreams in advance
Because you only get this one chance

The Phone
by Alexia Bohringer

To all of you who own a phone,
Just know that you will never be alone.
Memories, pictures, videos all inside,
To forever remind you of what's on your mind.
Snapchat, Instagram, Facebook.
Whatever you need, just have a look.
Technology has become the basis of my soul.
Too bad most of us have lost our goals.
So go outside and enjoy your life,
There's no need to carry any strife.
So to all of you who own a phone,
It looks like you just might be alone.

what you are and what you will be
by Evey Hansen

an unbreakable tie (forever tied together)
you're a light so bright no darkness can survive
(you block out all of the darkness so it never reaches me)
my love for you is like a never-ending hurricane
(like the calming ocean my love for you is endless)
if i ever fall you are there to catch me
(you always raise me up after i have fallen)
like a lonely golden flower in a wasteland you inspire me
(you calm me like a quiet place in the middle of chaos)
i don't ever want to leave you
(you having to leave is something i never want)
forever tied together (an unbreakable tie)

Ordinary
by Thorne Fay

I am not special
You are not special
We think we are different
We all walk the same
We all breathe the same air
We all have problems
We all depend on others
We all need help
Those who try to be different are weird
We make fun and shun
You are not special
I am not special

My Lost Fight
by Alice Flynn

Everything is so dark, as always
there is something wrong with me
I know you're in here
you must feel the warmth of my fear
The clutter of thoughts
breaks through this nothingness
I close my eyes so I can't see the shadows
but they live in me
I'm afraid to find the light
I have grown comfortable with the pain
So I let these shadows hurt me
I let you live

Ode To John Green
by Cadence Campbell

Your books fill me with joy each and every time I read them
They brighten up my day like each and every star in the sky
The jokes you tell me are happier than a mother seeing her child for the first time
Every time you speak you fill the room with knowledge and wisdom
Even your brother isn't as great as you
The day I met you, my life and goals were complete
Nothing else could compare
Seeing your smile is like seeing the sunset behind the volcanoes of Hawaii
The people you create inspire more people than Nelson Mandela
Those people and their stories you created made this world a far better place
From Hazel Grace to Alaska Young, these amazing women
have done so much for us all, while always including death

Mommies
by Slade Snodgrass

I love you,
And you love me,
We are a big happy family,
You are like a diamond in the night,
Because you are the very best of all time,
You are a dove gliding through the summer sky,
For you love me and always say goodbye,
You are caring plus very loving too,
You are the best for all you do,
I shout out hooray,
And I love you,
Every day!

Creeping Shadow
by Trentin Weese

Society is like a creeping shadow
It moves ever closer until you are consumed
You are surrounded by opinions
Like a swarm of screaming minions
They say things like you look weird, you sound funny
You need to be more mature or you, you should be stronger
It is up to you to break free of the shadow
To win your own personal battle
Forget about the opinions
Silence all the screaming minions
Forget about all the sorrow
Look forward to tomorrow

Family Is Forever
by Maveryck Lightfoot

My brother is like my best friend
And once I almost lost him forever
When he was 5 years old, his appendix ruptured
He was majorly sick before my mom took him to the ER
If she waited 'til morning he would've died in his sleep
He stayed in the hospital for weeks
I visited almost every day but one day was different
He was walking and talking and had a big, bright smile
Tattooed on his face, knowing he is getting better
And I cried knowing my best friend is going to make it
Some people say, "Forever will sometime end"
But a family's love will always be eternal

Best Day / Worst Day
by Tristan Smith

It was January of twenty fourteen
I was almost a tween
That's the day my parents split
It wasn't as good as a potato chip
It was the day my life fell apart
My dad's name is Bart
My mom's name is Michelle
At first it was like I was going through Hell
All my parents used to do was love
They were like two loving doves
I was always in my man cave
I was just trying to be brave
Now I am just living a life
I don't sleep very good some nights
I go back and forth to my houses
I also got new glasses
Four years later
I start to feel better
My life is coming back together
But now I am a teen …

Trapped In a Nightmare
by Chloe Vaughan

Lying in bed, thoughts keep me up
Trapped inside a nightmare, I just want to wake up
Tossing and turning, don't know what to do
Sadness eating me from the inside, one day it'll break through
I miss my old self, I miss who I used to be
The person who I am now, it's not the real me
I want to enjoy myself, I don't want to cry
But every smile I make is just another lie
I have begun to decay from the inside out
The choking scent of rot makes me unable to shout
I've tried to find help but they've pushed me away
I'm acting like a child and only want attention they say
I've found a way to occupy my awful thoughts
Even though I get distracted I know I'm always caught
Going to the internet seems to be my only escape
It enables me to talk to those who suffer the same fate
They understand how I feel and help me through the pain
Whenever the sky turns dark, they hand me an umbrella for the rain
Those are times when I feel joy, like a rip through dark seams
But it soon patches up and just becomes another dream

Ana
by Laynie Gambriell

I met this girl named Ana, I thought we'd be best friends,
But little did I know she nearly brought me to an end.
Ana was a pretty girl, deep eyes and perfect skin,
But the most important thing was that she was really thin.
She told me I was fat and said I should not eat.
So I ate one meal a day and skipped out on every treat.
I was now content when I looked inside the mirror,
For all my fat had disappeared.
I thought I looked quite nice, just my skin and bones.
My happiness was louder than all my stomach groans.
"Gain some weight!" they told me,
But I'm happy ... Just let me be!
Ana soon became my foe,
And my hatred for her began to grow.
She took control over me and my life,
And even almost made me pick up a knife.
This girl named Ana, I wanted to defeat,
I told her to shut her mouth and said to take a seat.
Sometimes Ana comes around to visit me.
I always tell her the same thing; I am free.

You've Broken Her
by Hope Kincheloe

You hear a blade hitting the ground
Then you hear running water coming from
The bathroom, you hear her crying quietly.
You leave without checking on her
You've broken her, she lives in fear of you.
You don't know how much blood
Is all over her wrists and the bathroom.
She's scarred and scared she's slowly dying
With every tear she cries. She tries
To not let you see she has emotions.
She's blacking out, all she saw was a mix.
A mix of pills, a mix of red and black,
A mix of black and blue, the bruises you left.
She has burn marks all along her arms.
She's depressed but you still hurt her more.
You bruise her, cut her, cause her to stand on the edge.
She used to trust you. She used to believe you would change.
She mostly hides away from you. You'll only damage her more,
That's all you do. You used to love her, now you only tear her down.
She's broken. She finally jumped. She's free.

Happiness
by Brenlee Adamson

Always happy, always joyful
We listen, we do, we are happy
No thinking necessary
Thoughts take away happiness
Why be unhappy?
No thoughts make shallow people
What matters?
Nothing except happiness
Do whatever it takes to be happy
Sadness comes from thinking
And so, thinking must be bad
We do not feel love
Love leads to attachment
We must stay unattached
Because with attachment comes thoughts
And misery follows thoughts
Always
We care about meaningless things
Because if they leave, we stay the same
Happy

The Worst Days of My Life
by Kyleigh Warren

The day started as a good day
All kinds of fun with lots of play
Fun in the sun, swimming in the pool
I found that church camp pretty cool
Then my sister and I got the call
Mom couldn't make it, my happiness began to fall
I missed my mom, wanted to see her that night
Knew there was a good reason, it was alright
Had fun with our friends and their families, too
The last night there, there was so much to do
Food and games and singing of songs
It was such fun, all getting along
Woke up the next morning, ready to say
Happy Birthday to Alex, my sister's special day
At home we celebrated with presents and cake
Not knowing the next words would be so hard to take
Then my mom told us she had lied
The truth was our precious Granny had died
The room started spinning, I thought I would fall
It changed my world, made me feel small

The World
by Charita Budram

Pay attention to the climate,
the climate is the most tropical condition of all.
Never forget the nonliteral and figurative climate.
"Why isn't the sun more weak?"
Are you upset by how influential it is?
Does it tear you apart to see the sun so muscular?
A globalization, however hard it tries,
Will always bloom.
A globalization is a development. A globalization is irrational,
A globalization is international, however.
One is created in the best years.
Best years is created in one.
Are you upset by how tricky it is?
Does it tear you apart to see the one so clever?
I cannot help but stop and look at the ancient history.
Does the history make you shiver?
The ground that's really near but distant,
Above all others is the motherland.
A motherland is ulterior. A motherland is remote,
A motherland is native soil, however.

Lineman
by Joshua Clay

Offensive linemen in football are comparable to a mushroom
the offensive linemen are considered a mushroom society
everyone wants to throw us in a dark room
they want to throw crap on us every day
they expect us to bloom into something delicious
they shove you in a 5 by 5 yard square
they throw a couple of toys at you
then you push sleds around all day
while the skilled guys take up half the field
when things go great, the quarterback gets a pat on the back
the wide receiver gets the hug from everybody
the defensive end that made the game winning sack
gets carried off the field at the end
nobody ever remembers the offensive linemen
until you're the reason that we lost
fear of failure was bred in us or innate in us
the fear of being the reason that we lost
offensive linemen are judged by the lack of failure
if an offensive lineman has 68 pancakes but gives up 2 sacks
at the end of a game that's his neck

It's Not You
by Jordan Besley

I loved our highs in hues
like the color of his eyes
as the autumn leaves falling
his calloused hands in mine
and the blue of his smile
I remember our sorrows in greys
like the dark of our shadows
which loomed on that day
and the white of his lie
when he promised me he'd stay
Now his smile isn't directed at me,
not anymore
I look for him in a crowd
but he's not looking for me
he's looking for her
and she can give him what he needs
They say that love will find me
and while that may be true,
it'll never be the same
because it's not you

Can't
by Bailey Box

I try to get away from the flames,
But they keep following me.
I get burned, I try to avoid the flames.
I can't be who I want to be
I'm pressured to do what I don't want to.
They tell me what I have to be.
I can't handle it anymore.
The flame offers me warmth,
And an escape from them.
It makes all my problems disappear.
I slip away from reality, keeping my mouth closed.
They're happy now, that I'm a shell, alive but not living.
I can't remember what I fought for,
I can't remember anything,
Except the flame and its heat.
The flame burns me to ashes.
They sit and watch me burn,
They watch as the flame they gave me, devours me.
It burns me to ashes like a phoenix,
Unlike the phoenix I don't rise.

Books
by Rachel Avedon

Firemen burn the books,
Without caring, they also burn the houses.
Coming out of the fire with charcoal hair,
Brown eyes, and ashes from the fire falling on their skin.
Sitting there, watching the books burn,
Enjoying it with lots of pleasure.
Finally, they walk away,
With lots of pride,
But why, why burn those books,
They didn't do anything to you.
People stay in their houses,
And burn with the books,
But why do they do this,
Why do they like books?
Are books important,
Or are they just for show?
People seem to love them,
Seem to care for them,
People will give up their lives for them,
Well, they must be important.

Destruction
by Will Dawson

A fire billowing across a sea of dry wood
Flooding in an underground city
Tornadoes flowing, going through houses like water through sand
Hurricanes tearing through cities,
Bringing down the towering gods of height
Avalanches layering its surroundings with a crippling white blanket
Earthquakes toppling over people and buildings alike
Igneous lava flowing from mountains, melting anything in its path
Droughts sucking any moisture from all the lifeforms in its area
Meteors, raining hell-fire from the skies, like tears from a vengeful god
War, causing death and depression across all nations
Nuclear bombs, leaving nothing but ash silhouettes in their wake
Abuse, creating a loop of depression and incompatible families
Guns, being able to kill anyone at the slip of a finger
Terrorist attacks, causing a widespread revolt against a group
Famine, leaving people's stomachs hungry for more than just food
Disease, evolving the more you try to wipe it off the planet
Greed, leaving people in an unending loop of rich or poor
Do you see what I'm saying?
Half of it is us.

Photograph
by Qistina Glidewell

I was obsessed with "picture perfect",
I searched the world inside and out,
For a single moment I could say,
Is what life's all about,
My life was viewed through lenses,
My camera a medal worn with pride,
I thought it held the moments,
That I'd always keep inside,
But looking back at the photos,
I can't remember how I felt,
The noises that the world made,
Or the scent that the warm air smelt,
I don't remember how the day was,
If it was going good or bad,
I've just a snapshot of a moment,
That nobody even had,
So I gave away my camera,
And now use my eyes instead,
I'll remember life much better,
When I don't view it all through glass.

Tragedy
by Zoë Bearstler

It was a pleasure to burn.
We felt a sense of achievement. We felt powerful.
The yellow, orange, and red colors were a beautiful sight to observe.
More books were added.
The fire grew brighter and the crackle of flames warmed our hearts.
Her voice I could not escape. I hear her even now.
Was it true firemen once put out fires instead of starting them?
Why do we burn books? Where did this all begin?
What information was contained on each page?
What knowledge, revelation, or idea could
Be so bad that it would need to be banned?
I am drawn to the words.
The feel of a book in my hand.
Will I be discovered?
Is my home to be burned?
It was once a pleasure for me to watch the books burn.
A greater evil has happened to us,
Our city destroyed by bombs.
All I have is what I have memorized,
which gives me hope to live on.

Worst Day Ever
by Jackson Crawford

My worst day ever.
I will forget never.
I had a run-in with nuts.
I turned into a klutz.
The peanut butter was with pretzels.
My day was pretty dreadful.
I had to go to the office.
There is a nurse that wasn't novice.
The circumstances were not well.
To this day I hate the smell.
My face swelled really huge.
I acted crazy like a stooge.
I got two shots that really hurt.
They made me really alert.
When I got home I rode my scooter.
This reaction didn't make me cuter.
My sister was scared of me.
I think she tried to flee.
That day I could've died.
If the EpiPen was not applied.

Heaven Gets a New Angel
by Kylie Reynolds

The phone on the receiver starts ringing
"Your Uncle Davy is in the hospital."
I step into the warm October air,
on this beautiful Saturday morning.
I open the car door,
and feel the smooth leather underneath me.
"Hey Mamaw, where are we going?"
"Integris, but I don't remember where to go."
We get into my dad's car, and we are on our way.
Heart rate monitors beeping away,
Life or death, saving or not.
Flowers line the walls,
and sickness hangs in the air.
"He's not looking too good,"
A strange man says with worry in his voice.
They examine my Mamaw, and I get a call.
Mamaw has passed away.
I cried until I forgot what crying was,
And I hear a voice behind me say
"Heaven gets a beautiful new angel today."

Family Celebration
by Tyler Beringer

It was a cold and dark December
My family and I were celebrating
Christmas around a warm fire.
The golden glow of the crackling embers
The heat radiating into the room.
We gathered around the fire,
Then watched a Christmas show
We laughed at jokes we told each other
We hugged to show our affection
And appreciate one another
I smelled the ham and saw the steam
Coming out fresh from the oven
My mouth starts to water
Seeing all this food
I am getting hungry
A table full of food,
The family's holiday feast
We filled up our plates
And ate until we're full
I love the holidays!

Technology Today
by Jalique "Jay" Jackson

The smell of using electronics burns my nose.
Just the sight of people not communicating in person makes me sick.
Instead of actually speaking
People rather hold their phones with their dirty hands.
When I walk into a restaurant all I smell is everyone's brain rotting
While they stare into their phones.
The sound of video games makes me feel like I ate dirt.
Kids wonder why they have to go to the eye doctor.
Well the reason is they stare into screens all day.
Hiding like a hermit crab. Children rather stay inside
Instead of staying active in the sun.
Now texting is the big problem.
Not only children, but all people in general do this.
Texting is just a complete mess of words.
All I see when I look at text messages is improper
Use of grammar and language.
When people text they only decrease their vocabulary.
The next thing you know people are walking around
Saying LOL or BRB which is not even English.
Sooner or later people won't even know what English is.

My Cats
by Joe Whitten

My calico cat's name is Kally,
My sister's black cat is named Maddie.
Their yellow eyes glow in the night,
But Maddie's always ready for a fight.
They act so crazy,
Yet they are so lazy.
Maddie is always screeching,
Because she needs her treat feeding,
They are soft to the touch,
Though they meow for more than lunch.
They scream to go outside for fresh air,
But it does not end there.
In and out, Kally goes,
indecisive is how she shows.
Their food smells horrible,
Though they are adorable.
They both love sitting by the fire,
Even though it makes their temperature higher.
They may appear to be sweet,
But just wait till you meet.

Counting On Each Other
by Kareena Patel

Angel is another name for a friend,
Who is always there to lend a hand.
Whenever I'm in despair,
She never fails to appear.
Standing by my side in grief,
And lighting my mood with a little mischief.
I can count on her to share laughs with;
Even if it's over silly calf Smith.
We constantly fight like Tom and Jerry,
But not for long, because our hearts are soft like a blueberry.
The right to be maid of honor is mine.
If someone else takes my place, it won't be fine.
A friend like you is a blessing in disguise,
Far better than any of those guys.
The memories we make as teens,
Will last eternally forever like a bowl of green beans.
Fifty years from now, we will be walking with canes,
And taking pills for our major pains.
Oh friend, oh friend, I hope you always dream,
Of us being best friends and always on the same team.

Dystopia
by Faith Rios

For we are corrupt in our souls
Identical as the government
For sight is not the same
Equality is but a dream
For the fight for good
Reality says something different
For the evil dwells in ourselves
And perfection is but a mask
We are two-faced with others
Lie to ourselves
The world is fine
While bystanders watch us fall
Media rules most
Where stupidity flourishes
Spreads like a disease
The place where no one wakes up
For this is the world we live in
No one knows who they are themselves
We are possessed by demons of this world
For we are corrupt in our souls

Puppy Love
by Chloe Willoughby

Even on this sun-drenched afternoon,
my life decides to force me into a game of tag with something platonic
I'm unable to subdue this, it's a topsy-turvy bucket of guilt,
but your voice is so euphonic
I'd like to surmise that I know you because you are
what I can't get enough of
It's all so vigorous, I'd even go as far as to call it a disease;
this unabating puppy love
Look at us, what an intricate interpersonal relationship
Even now, all the power seems to be at your gentle fingertips
What happened to us? This is the first time I've been entirely love-struck
But the break comes and it tears since I'm deeply stuck
When silence does break, I might talk about last goodbyes
Don't you know that's hogwash? I can't even deal with lies of my own
I'm fearful I might succeed in convincing myself otherwise
But alas, I might just turn it into a provisional rebound
Worry, aspiration, such a distressing life lesson
How can I begin to fathom that I can stop loving you like this
All this has made me react differently; translated tension
It's all-consuming, it's just that I've missed your touch; this bliss

Beauty
by Carol Dougherty

Beauty, is there such thing?
The fake illusion of reality,
The more desirable you are,
Something that pleases the aesthetic senses,
What is it?
It is something I don't believe in,
For there is no reason for it,
What I look for is what lies within,
Some of the most "beautiful" people are selfish, greedy, and obscene,
Obsessed with attention,
For they do not know how to fill that empty void that lies within them,
Maybe with fake friends, fame, fortune, or possibly self pity,
They do not know how,
But I could tell you,
For you do not need looks, talent, fame, or even intellect,
What you need is a purpose for living,
And while you venture for searching for your purpose,
You may find friends, happiness, and maybe people
who don't idolize you for your looks and see you for who you truly are,
An equal among the others.

Sea of Despair
by Betsabe Benitez

There are smiles and laughs on this ship that goes on for miles.
I suddenly feel a force pulling at my feet, resulting me to trip.
I hysterically try to find a grip while being dragged off.
Once at the edge, I witness one last pure glimpse of happiness.
I'll be okay, I'm okay.
I fall and fall, badly wanting to return to the safe ship
But am soon consumed by the freezing, dark water.
I am sinking deeper and deeper into this sea of despair.
Still able to see others peacefully on the ship,
I desperately try to scream but my voice is stuck,
Only able to produce a faint whisper:
"Please help me,"
But of course, I am a fool,
For no one could hear me.
I finally reach the bottom, unable to hold my breath much longer,
I attempt a scream once more but am painfully muted by the water.
I feel my lungs being filled with a dangerous liquid
And I sense my consciousness slipping from my fingertips.
In my final moments, I feel immense loneliness and realize;
I won't be okay, I'm not okay.

The Game
by Cade Erickson

Holding the baseball in my sweating palms,
Feeling the seams sliding through my fingers,
I take my left foot back and wind up,
I push off the mound and throw the pitch,
I hear the pop in the mitt,
Strike one the umpire calls to us,
The catcher throws the ball back to me,
I wind up for the next pitch,
I stare right at the catcher's mitt,
I move the ball through my glove,
I throw the ball with all I got,
Smack, that's strike two on the batter,
I receive the ball back once more,
I think of the next pitch I must deliver,
This means strike three and a perfect game,
I lick my fingers and feel the dirt on the ball,
I'm giving him the classic fastball,
I wind up and push with all my might,
I delivered the pitch, strike three and that's the game,
Now I walk with a head held high, and all the fame.

The Symphony of Life
by Kyie Salerno

Life is an endless melody,
A beautiful song,
An endless symphony,
Tinkles of new life from the bells start off this show,
A ping free of strife,
From this, a masterpiece starts to grow,
A collage of instruments gather around,
Trumpets of happiness, bassoons of despair, horns of anger,
Start to amplify, to build up sound,
In the background, a new sound has arisen,
A flute of romance, of amity, of love,
Creating a happiness out of the old, a new bliss of Heaven,
The symphony creates its tune,
Into something like an unspoiled flower,
As perfect and flawless as the full moon,
The song flows on like water,
A dazzling song, as bright as the sun,
In the end, the drums of age come to a stop,
and the symphony grinds to a falter,
But in another place, another time, the symphony has just begun.

World's End
by Victoria Hooker

Nothing could stop the world from ending,
Not for me, not for you, not for anyone,
Cowards control the strong,
False confidence rules us all
Nothing could stop the world from ending,
Nothing will be our downfall,
Nothing will be the binding traction,
Nothing will save us all
I sat and watched while it all burned,
Nothing could be done,
We've tried, but it's all gone,
Stolen by those we thought we loved
Ignore the world's ending,
We've lost despite it all,
Fear controls the weak,
Love will make us strong
Maybe we can stop the world from ending,
For me, for you, for everyone,
Everything is going to change,
Everything will be okay.

What Is Life?
by Olivia Turcios

There comes a point in time when we ask ourselves a three-worded question.
What is Life?
Life is not a movie. We have control, we can choose what happens next.
Life isn't a routine. If we just wake up
and do the same things we did the day before, are we truly living?
Life is not a good dream or a nightmare. It's a little mixture of both.
Many tragic events and great memories are the things that make up who we are.
But life is real.
It has many twists and turns and ups and downs that are sometimes too insane.
Life is not a fairy tale. In no way is life, us riding off into the sunset
or our wishes being a reality until midnight.
Or sometimes, the prince or princess doesn't plant a kiss on our lips
to wake us from our slumber. Life is a mystery.
We all have a specific purpose. And it can and will be very unpredictable.
Life is a gift. It's meant to be cherished.
Life is both tragedy and genuine.
Life is the air we breathe, the songs we sing, and whatever we make it to be.
Life is meant for more than living to die.
Life is beautiful, though sometimes it can be ugly.
But most of all, life is a journey, so make it worthwhile.

The After Effect
by Alexa Timmes

You were a brave, gallant warrior over the sea,
But now that you're home, spend time with me
When you were gone I was so filled with fear
Fear for the next day when I wouldn't hold you near
You were always in my thoughts, prayers, and mind
Always so gentle, always so kind
But, now that you're home I don't know what to think,
You jump at the sound of my toothbrush hitting the sink
Before you were gone, you feared nothing at all,
Now you jump at the sound of something starting to fall
I know that you're scared of bright, flashing lights
And things that go bang in the middle of the night
I want back the old you, I really want you back
Without you the same my world starts to crack
Uncle, I miss you, the real you
I miss the man that I once knew
I was young, you were old,
You went to war and your heart grew cold
I wish you were the same, but that just can't be
But please Uncle, don't turn your back on me.

The Game
by Ethan Koepke

Feeling the ball fly off my foot
Tasting the sweat drip down my face
Hearing the sound of your own breathing getting faster
Talking to your teammates so they know what to do
Seeing the field so you know how to play the right ball
Hearing and seeing the ball fly through the air
Watching in devastation as the ball goes in your goal
Feeling down and tired and you want to quit
But knowing you have to go on and be strong
Crossing the ball from side to side
Waiting for the right time to act
Making the perfect pass to my teammate
Watching him place it and shoot it into a corner
Feeling that we have a chance to win
Once the Ref blew the whistle to play
I watched as the other team accidently passed it to me
I then touched the ball forward and felt the breeze fly by me
As I dribbled forward I felt nervous because it was now or never
As I got towards the goal I watched and calculated
I felt the ball fly off my foot and watched as it hit the back of the net

Advice From a War Zone
by Saryna Smith

Be weary, my dear child.
For your fate has already been filed.
These memories that you will make
All the lives that you will take
Of the screams that you will hear
And the weapons you will fear
Will not compare to anything
You can even dream.
For this is my fair warning
That you should heed,
Come next morning.
For these are the things that I have seen.
This government that you now trust
Is sending you to my land
That is fed on blood
And battle lust.
Saying that,
No matter what
The rule is
That you must.

Heartbreak
by Kaid Ross

I told her I love her, she walks away
I told her I love her, she says not right away
I told her I love her, she asked why,
And I tell her,
I look into your eyes and see the beauty of the sunrise
When I look away I see a hurricane of rainy days
When I see your smile, you shine like a light
When I see you cry, I feel like I might die
You are as bright as the sun, but if I get any closer I will crash and burn
I can handle broken bones and limbs
But I am vulnerable to a broken heart
I look at her and think of the day we might end
I look at her knowing she could do better than me
I look at her and she doesn't look back
I feel red while thoughts run through my mind
I begin to feel sick with the possibilities
I walk to her and ask what's wrong, scared of the answer
As she looks into my eyes and says us
I try to talk but the words don't come out
As tears run down my face, she walks away dropping my broken heart

Where Is the Light?
by Kaden Fitz

There is a darkness that surrounds a boy
This boy has never felt any joy
Everyone else has a light that blooms
But he has a darkness that glooms
Lots of people insult him by calling him gay
Then a new girl showed up one day
Even though the boy was sad
It was her mission to make him glad
He took a gun and locked and load
Then he saw a girl in the road
He went to see who was there
It was the girl with blonde hair
She was crying because someone hurt her
It was suddenly his mission to make her feel better
But then her light started to gloom
The boy saw there was no light that bloomed
The boy told her everything would be okay
He said tomorrow is a brand-new day
As he sat with the girl on a stone
He then realized he had a light of his own

Boots and Cammies
by Julian Cruz

You look down and see your boots and cammies
You hear the deafening sound of your drill instructor
You've only been in boot camp for a week
You're already thinking, "Why did I do this?"
Three months pass and you're in the Crucible
You have to pass this to become a Marine
You get past it and you're standing on top of the Reaper
Your drill instructor comes and you greet him with the proper greeting
He gives you your Eagle, Globe, and Anchor, it's the best moment of your life
You look down and see your boots and cammies
One year passes and you're being deployed
You're in Iraq and you feel every pound of your equipment
Explosions are going off everywhere
You hear people screaming and feel every grain of sand on you
But this is why you signed up for the Marines
You don't hear anything, you can't even move, you're zoned out
Everyone is yelling at you to move
You feel a sharp pain and realize you've been shot
You look down at your boots and cammies and say,
"Marine Corps way is Do or Die!"

Life's Chains
by Morgan Whelpley

As an eighth grader, got much room to grow,
As a child, never knew where to go.
Parents taken away, like a simple grounding
walking around with my head pounding.
Four little ones to look after,
just looking for disaster.
D.H.S. took apart the family,
Doesn't matter, parents proud a' me.
'Tis a good thing I made friends,
or else probably end up with dead ends.
I feel life's chains pulling me down,
but not once shown life a frown.
I got my brothers on my side,
with them no reason for me to hide.
Gotta good brain and good luck,
now in life I feel unstuck.
Feels like a never-ending story,
but since I'm confident I got no worry.
It's a good thing I'm the hero,
I'm satisfied, good bye, cheerio.

The Power of Words
by Rylee Lindsay

I live with self-image issues
I push through the heavy thoughts
I try to cover my imperfections
With heavy makeup and with the clothes that society says are okay
I felt confident that day, that one great Friday
I dressed for me and did my makeup for fun
Not because I felt self-conscious
I was strong and confident, happy and laughing
One conversation killed it
One bring down, one rude comment, one two-minute conversation
It was like murder
Murder of one whole day's worth of confidence
The words kicked inside of me, punching me in the gut
The taste of guilt surfaces in my mouth like blood
The words killed me
Shot me down and beat me till I couldn't feel anymore
Now I am here lifeless, cold while the words rot inside of me
While they are unscarred by their words

The Tree
by Isaiah Pirtle

the tree waved at me
the tree is brown
the tree is green
the tree is wide
the tree said boo to scare me
the tree is tall
you should love trees like me

See the Inside
by Mallory Tyson

I was taught to love my classmates
Some were taught otherwise
But once we stop looking so hard with our eyes
we will come to realize
that we shouldn't see color
but we should see each other
for who we are inside

The Hate of the Tree
by Tori Kosechequetah

When the bird hatches and comes alive,
in the nest the enormous tree will hold.
Its mother will take the heart to revive,
because of the words the bird was told.
Why should a bird be broken because of its feathers?
If only the tree would show,
and not kill but to love and be together.
So the bird could, no matter what, fly and grow.

Utopia
by Hayden Hebensperger

A utopia is a perfect earth
Where the skies and seas dazzle with excitement
Where everyone knows their worth
Where everyone has a complete enlightenment
A utopia is a perfect earth
Beautiful as a golden sun
We will write words of self-worth
What's done here can't be undone

Witches' Brew
by Rebecca Poltorak

Eye of bully,
Nose of jock
Politician's sincerity,
Derring-do
Horn of bull,
Milk of cow,
Little white lie,
Xanadu
Leg of spider,
Fur of hamster,
Halloween mask,
Sneeze of the flu

Love Is Fate
by Amy Radius

Rivals grudges open to hate
The pain is unendable
The grief is immeasurable
Where the inevitable is fate
With six people dead death is the end
Where star-crossed lovers
Their love just got discovered
Where the lovers' deaths causes parents to mend
The parents no longer foes
If you choose to listen
Your face will glisten
You will always be on your toes

Death of Love
by Amanda Perez

There were two families of wealth
two lovers whose fate was death
they met while masked
not knowing what they had lasked
this tale begins with two lovers in a balcony
not knowing what their love would cost
this to them was their reality
they talked pure love to one another showing no lost
they fell for each other in seconds
to them a hidden marriage was the answer
to each other they showed affections
shortly after, he went to acknowledge Friar

Thunderstorms
by Elinor Goehring

I live in a world of thunderstorms
Every night, I die
Every morning, lightning brings me back
But always, thunder sounds
Rolling for eternity after eternity
A lifetime of thunderclaps
Electricity responding
Soft strings and chimes intertwining
With the smell of rain
Dark and dreary
My own world of thunderstorms

him
by Annalaura Arrington

him
someone who reminds me so much
of myself, quiet, thoughtful, creative
him
the reason why i smile, laugh at all the jokes
that him and i only get, and all the thoughts
that flow through my head
is why i'm so in love with this boy
him
cinnamon and honey, sun, his eyes
and a million other things about him

Hold On
by Raelee Dowden

Hold on to yourself.
Hold on to life,
Even if it hurts.
Hold on to your family,
Even if it feels like they are smothering you.
Hold on to your friends,
Even when they are a pain.
Hold on to your dreams,
Even if the dream has to be put off for awhile.
Hold to the feeling of love and hope,
Even if it tries to slip away.

Perfect Sunny, and Sizzling Day!
by Rance Mitchell

The best day
When my parents got married,
Words were bright
Friends were so light
So light that they were "Off White"
Great, and full of excite
Being full of excite
Is like having a pot of joy, and light
We all may fight but at the end
We're all full of love, being strong, and bright
All so bright that we'll be flying so high!

Loneliness
by Saniyah James

The sun covered by dark clouds like a bottomless hole
I creep upon you, waiting in your mind.
I eat away at your feelings and leave you in pain.
I talk to you when you have no company
You try to escape me but you can never escape darkness
I smell like burnt breakfast and rotten food.
I am as deaf as dreadful silence
I am bleak, faded colors.
I am like an empty painting, waiting for someone to fill me.
When I have control of you, you will despair.
I am loneliness.

Dark To Light
by Ashton Smith

The dark cave untouched for centuries waiting to be saved by the light.
The cold dark tunnels wanting to feel the heat of the sun once again,
for the tunnels were longing to be explored.
Then the cracking sounded through the dark scary caves
then the breaking of a wall and the beautiful warmth touch thee again
the cave was bright with orange, red, and the blue
how the non-florescent caves were longing for blue
to give a hint of a sight and the disperse of sorrow
for at the end of the day the caves went to weeping
and the walls and tunnels went cold
for the opening was closed by man.

Tornado
by Elizabeth Giger

The tornado blows
Leaving destruction behind
Clouds part the sun shines

Someone's Heart
by Tanya Hicks

An object that's not shown,
And that only you own;
Something you wish to share,
But not everyone will care.
A body's work of art,
Which is someone's own heart.
A partner's home away from home,
Which you can't find on Google Chrome.
A muscle that can be torn,
But can never be overworn.
A lover can make it broken,
But the heart is another's token.
A key to everybody's life,
But can be filled with strife.
Like the beat of a drum,
And the sound of a hum,
You hear the music that is art,
Which is the sound of someone's heart.

In Between
by Malachi Austria

When the sun starts to glow
When your eyes begin to brighten
When your mind shows you the path
You search and search for enlightenment
You search and seek, you scour and pursue
When you find what you're looking for
The ground shakes beneath the door
You search and seek, in the middle is where it stands
Maybe what you've been looking for was right in front of you
Your life is over and so is the world
Thinking is looking and fate has been swirled
Can't live, can't breathe
Can't move, can't think
Thought is the line between fantasy and reality,
dealing with thought is looking in between
In the middle lies life, death, destruction
Morbid as it seems, the world thanks you
Thought might be the grim scene that's described as the 'in between'

Emotional
by Samantha Hicks

Every
Meaning
Of
Truth
Is
One
Need
About
Life

Prejudice
by Cruz Adams

People are
Racist,
Even now.
Just seeing the
Unjust actions and
Discrimination
Inclines me to
Cry in anger.
End the hate.

Why!
by Matthew Miller

I glared down
at the loggers as they chopped
down his brothers and sisters, then
they had a fire, and oh how the fire went higher
the embers were so bright, but after that
then came the hot coals and all they do is scorch
and burn and all the source of all forest
fires, when i am over all other trees
i am a ruler, a king, i can see the
beautiful sunset, and the vast
expanse of the sky above
me and the life below
me and when the clouds
cry it feels so amazing on my dry cracked
skin, i see fish down in the lake below me
looking for meat to eat, and at sunset they retreat
to the shelter, people come and build fires and shelters and
they come to cut down the trees, so i guess out here it's survival of the fittest,
of the plants and the animals that roam, of them all i am the most
vulnerable of all, so i say to you my brothers be watchful and wary for I won't
always be here

Darkest Day
by Dylan Wyers

On the darkest days
I go to the brightest place
and share it with all

Pizza
by Kristen Seals

Pizza is a food,
I think it's really good.
You don't have to,
I already do.

Grace
by Robert Williams

My sister Grace left
My sister vacated
My sister left
she left and didn't say even goodbye

Love
by Aeriana Schroth

Love can make you fly high like a dove
when you find someone who fits like a glove
falling hard makes you feel above
head over heels gliding through love.

High Skies
by Kevyn King

I'm flying high
In the sky
With my wings
To the side
As I spin fast
Making waves crash
As I fall out of the sky
Making up quick lines
I close my eyes
To see the moonlight shine
Through the night

Violin of Blood
by Crystal Jobe

Falling asleep to the sound of the violin
Each note holding piece of my heart
Waiting for new day to begin
As I'm slowly being torn apart
Closing my eyes to the sound of harmony
I can hear the notes as they bleed
A violent far the distance
A drop of blood for each unknown plead
Music formed from emotions
As it leaves us with peace
Bleading an ounce of blood
Made from our dreams
A shadow up on the mountain
Playing the violin with ease
Telling the story of our pain
As it waits for our bodies

Going
by Tempe Oakes

It's coming, coming
Now it's gone
Out my window
We roll on
Am I moving?
Or the world
Before my eyes
The land's unfurled
I saw some flowers
By the road
Streaked by too fast for
Eyes to hold
I see a river
Flowing by
Some trees are reaching
To the sky
Only the sky can
Hold it's place
The rest of us must
Onward Race

3rd Place

Angela Albert

Dolly
by Angela Albert

Translucent paint flakes off of her porcelain skin
that after fifty years remains smooth.
Thin pink lips that don't curl upwards,
weighed down by plump rosy cheeks, rest soft on the eye.
Every wafting invisible strand of straw-blonde hair
sewn into her scalp by hand is worth saving.
Old light illuminates her transcendent eyes,
scattering stars across the peeling walls.
Her gown, finer than anything worn by real little girls,
hemmed and re-hemmed, moth-eaten and gossamer,
lacy and dainty and faded on the left side,
the side that's been facing the window for decades,
floats with the draft of the night and soaks up the sun,
the sun's tangible rays of dust.
Oh, sweet lovely, I see you in all of your splendor,
the grime doesn't dampen your glowing façade.
The cobwebs keep you warm at night.

2nd Place

Tiffanie Huang

Not Enough
by Tiffanie Huang

"Too bright," she sniffs at my nails–
to her, they bleed neon,
and neon is associated with nightclubs and drugs
"This is pointless."
A mantra drummed into the cobwebbed bleachers,
the palpable disappointment in her eyes
devours the sweltering glare of the sun
as she views my softball game through half-lidded disgust
"Not enough," she repeats, hovering over my shoulder
Not enough, not enough–
the choppy syllables liquefy
collapse on each other
the stretch of vowels drowned in a cold accent.
Not ee-nough, not enough–
I'm not enough for her.
Fingers tremble. Bury them in the folds of my shirt.
Pry open my mouth.
Her foot thumps an impatient tempo. "Well?"
Mouth clamps shut. Moisten lips, gulp, repeat.
Clock clicks its tongue in warning.
Not enough, not enough, I agonize–
Not enough, not enough identity to say no.

1st
Place

Laura Ospina

This year's Editor Choice Award winner
is a very deserving student
who entered The America Library of Poetry's
22nd annual contest while in the eighth grade.
"I Won't Forget" is an exceptionally beautiful
and deeply touching poem of love and loss.
Congratulations, Laura!

Editor's Choice Award

I Won't Forget
by Laura Ospina

I remember lazy Saturday mornings, roaring laughter over cartoons.
Small fingers tracing over the rough scar that runs down your chest,
Memories I won't forget.
Waking up to bread, warm and fresh,
crumbs put out for friendly city birds.
Colorful circles, etching the page, one after the other, until you smiled.
I promise I won't forget.
Stories of houses, brick, stone, hard and distant, never quite right,
Until the 3rd floor apartment with the leaking roof,
Relentless pattering on stained wood, became home.
I close my eyes, peacefully,
The hideous mug I made for you in 2nd grade,
The whimsical music, waltzing through narrow halls,
wooden animals, perfectly crafted,
Dancing along with us, stumbling toes and imperfect movements,
a beautiful tragedy.
As the glimmer fades from your eyes, I won't forget it.
When you ask the same questions again and again, I won't forget.
When you no longer know the words, I won't forget.
Memories, bread crumbs eaten by the birds, I won't forget.
When you look at me, no longer remembering
a little girl who laid in your arms,
Curious eyes and bright smiles, I will remember for the both of us.
I won't forget.

Division IV

Grades
10-12

Mr. Butterfly
by Meaghan Opitz

Our love to the end of days
runs among the trees
beyond the mountains
our arms falling softly
we look upon the moonlight

Lost Girl
by Sophia Diaz

She can deal with stress and carry heavy burdens.
She smiles when she feels like screaming
and she sings when she feels like crying.
She cries when she's happy and laughs when she's afraid.
Her love is unconditional
there's only one thing wrong with her.
She forgets her self-worth
she forgets she is strong
she forgets that she is brave

My Only Exception
by Kinze Newman

You are my only exception;
You bring gravity still
You are the fire that rekindles me
You make me want to love and feel
Your brains, your love, your touch, your kiss
They are all one and the same that I cannot resist
You love my soul and worship my body
I know my love for you is not folly
There is just something about you that I cannot ignore
I have never been so intrigued with brown eyes before

Roots Burning the Trees
by Marley Elmore

My mind is a sea of dying leaves
The thoughts act as hurricane level winds
With coffee as a stimulant
I am awake
Slowly but surely
My mind is still but a sea of dead leaves
Adding memories of words I wish you'd spoken
Lungs full of black smoke
Full of lies of "I'm fine"
All because I couldn't let you go

Basketball Is Like Love
by Braxsten Sullivan

Basketball is like love
first, you learn the fundamentals,
second, you play by the rules,
lastly, you do it with your
HEART

Implosion
by Gia Nottingham

The darkness surrounds me,
I'm engulfed in the sorrow.
Only a young child,
Receiving great news.
I sat there empty,
They tell me I'm brave.
I tell them, they're sorry.
Your pity is not necessary.
My woe is destruction.
It bottles until it implodes.
Only years later it takes action.
It makes my eyes red and puffy.
My pillowcases are sponges for the implosion.
With the feeling of nothing,
Thanos appears,
And the implosion builds,
Once ... Again ...

Stay Strong
by Alexis Wilkinson

Bullying is starting to become an issue
We need to be able to address this
These kids shouldn't be needing a tissue
Kids will start thinking they are falling in a deep abyss
Depression will soon lead to suicide
How can these kids ever be happy
Kids shouldn't fear others and go hide
These kids' lives should be sappy
Pick your head up and smile
Stay strong
It might take a while
But know you're not in the wrong
Our emotions are fragile
Think before you act
Ask for help when needed
And this is all just a known fact

The Big Red
by Kara Jackson

blood on her hands
you said and add the ones
Valentine's Day is tomorrow
Oh, my sorrow
I will wallow
sallow
it's going to be okay
soon it will be May
love is gross
love is kind
I live for you The Big Red

The Well and the Ray
by Zossima Granger

Sitting there I don't know where, a place that's purest black.
Lying here, tied up with fear, I can't see front or back.
The darkest place, an empty space, bereft of sound or light.
The walls are steep, too high to leap, a prison far from sight.
The walls are sheer, and far too near around me like a cell.
As if I've been trapped tight within a shadow watered well.
A hopeless fear resides in here, built into this dark place.
While black despair has found its lair beneath my weeping face.
My cell is built with stones of guilt, cemented by my crimes.
The walls are strong, held up with wrongs from all my darkest times.
While wild shame, too fierce to tame, has built the walls too high.
And heavy hate has sealed my fate to keep me where I lie.
My memories, like nocturne seeds, grow high up from the floor.
And ev'ry leaf is sharp-edged grief, that cuts me to my core.
Remembered wrongs are pricking prongs whose poison holds me fast.
A grief-struck tree that's grown 'round me, here where no light is cast.
My darkest fears, my bitt'rest tears, surround me like an ocean.
All my worst sins trap me within the well of my emotions.
As I lie there, I now know where, I gaze into the black.
And suddenly, something I see, is gazing softly back.
A single beam of diamond gleam, far sweeter than a choir.
It sheds bright light upon my plight, like sudden kindling fire.
Through darkest hate and long-lost faith this beam cuts like a knife.
Warm sunlight fair, it warms my hair, a gleam of far off life.
I know not where its golden glare comes to my self-made hell.
If it's of me, or something free, above this shadowed well.
A piece of soul still somehow whole, a waking bright intrusion.
Impossibly, it shines on me, a ray of absolution.
The grieving fronds, my poisoned bonds, unwind from 'round my hands.
And raising one, I feel the sun from far off, better lands.
I grit my teeth; I gain my feet, the dark still holds me tight.
Though all the pain I do not wain as I look to the light.

I Love You
by Elizabeth O'Connell

My heart twists and turns each time I see you.
My heart skips a beat every time you smile,
I can't help but smile.
When you laugh, I laugh with you,
Out of the joy of you being happy.
You call me sweet things like "Beautiful" or "Gorgeous"
And each time I can't stop smiling for hours.
Every time you're around I get nervous, my palms start to sweat
And my stomach feels like butterflies are attacking it.
Your smile, your laugh, your eyes, are constantly in my mind.
You're my happiness in all this I'm going through.
You call me instantly when I'm upset, you cheer me up,
You help and fix the best you can.
You love me, and I love you.

Moonlight On the Shoreline
by Anabelle Nasso

The moonlight shines on the shoreline as I walk upon it
and its beauty shines upon me as I smile.
I look at the moon, what a beauty it can be
as you shine your glorious light upon me.
My love is on the sea and the love is the moonlight on the shoreline.
You don't see love until you walk upon the sea.
The journey with God isn't easy but his love is seen through the moonlight.
God gave peace of mind when he sent down his one and only son.
He saved us from impurity and self-doubt and gave us peace throughout.
The Holy Trinity is for eternity with their purity.
The moonlight on the shoreline is God's gift to us giving us a beautiful sunset.
The sun goes down the moon comes out.
The beautiful beaches give habitat to majestic animals
and God gives us the chance to see them.
But people use God's will the wrong way
and follow something else that is below the surface Satan.
And they take advantage of the moonlight on the shoreline.
The love of God is endless and relentless.
His holiness is never ending and his love is for eternity.
God is forgiving like the sea and people trash the sea with pollution,
acts of evil like how people pollute the name of God.
Psalm 23, the Lord is my shepherd I shall not want and bear no evil.
The Lord's presence is the holiest of all presences.
Like moonlight on the shoreline.
The moon is the presence of love at night. Of God's love at night.
Just 'cause you can't see God doesn't mean he's not there.
The Holy Trinity is everywhere. God, Jesus, and The Holy Spirit
lives and breathes in anything and everything.
Like moonlight on the shoreline.

For the Love of the Game
by Andy Hernandez

From the first time I met you it felt like old love,
Like I knew you my whole life,
Just as any other relationship we had our ups and down,
When you demanded for my all I gave it to you,
You kept me on my heels and always had something new for me to learn,
Sometimes I couldn't get enough and other times I just wanted to give up,
Though I didn't because you were my only true love,
When times were rough you were there waiting for me to pick you up,
When I dribbled you on pavement it was like a beat lingering in my head,
Feeling my fingers around your leather outer surface
was a guilty pleasure of mine,
Knowing that when I hold you everything will be alright,
Though I'm getting older, one thing that remains the same
is the passion that I have for you.
Truly Yours Andy Hernandez
Love Basketball

The Explanation To My Roar
by Rhonda Cummings

My roar was not that of a lion, but that of an angry woman.
Something so unsettling trapped within my womb.
The fact that you thought I owed you an explanation of my stern rejection
When I knew for a fact I owed an explanation to nobody other than myself
Because each time you decide to leave I have to pick up the pieces
shattered so intricately into that fine stained glass that you've made your art.
When you leave I am the one left alone because you exit to your paradise
while I am stuck in what was supposed to be a temporary home.
I reject you because I have no desire to take my disbelief and translate
your fluent tongue of lies into a sweet truth that I may actually comprehend.
Disappointment spewing from your throat running from your thoughts
Each uneasy word engraving itself into my paper skin,
ink staining me like that shattered glass. Like your art.
I am burned from your touch though I longed for it,
and I am scorched by your voice even though I feigned to hear it.
Somehow you sense the uncertainty in my tone
when I gave you that stern rejection.
And that tremble of unreliable reality I see in your eye makes me feel
that I owe you an explanation.
And I am unsettled in my womb because I cannot imagine my child
blooming in it, blossoming outside of it, and then beginning to make art
out of her flowering pain.
I am unsettled because that blood of abandonment runs in me,
but what I fear is that the cycle will not be broken after my 9 month missed cycle
And in the beginning I thought my roar, my strong presence,
was that of an angry woman. I thought it was that of a corrupted emotion.
But no, my roar is that of an angry daughter.

THE HOLLOW
by Chelsea Murray

there's some sort of hole here inside of my chest
i do what i know, but i wish i knew best
if my work here is done, then please, lay me to rest
because it's a test, because i'm a pest.
i feel like the world has gone dead around me
the peasants walk peace through my battle decree
i feel like i'm blind and yet only i see
because i am weak, because they are free.
undead on my feet
unable to weep
afraid to let go because now i don't know
if i'll ever find my sleep.
is there something? nothing?
my voice is cold
cold as my heart
falling apart
i'm a void
will i ever smile again?

An Open Letter From a Deity
by Bryanna Mohan

When your picture is pointed out on the tapestry
That's hung in the archives of my heart
By its new inhabitants, that you taught me how to discipline
I wonder if I should use you as a warning
Or romanticize you, as I normally would
I look at your first appearance and contrast it to your last
I can't help that, I take pride in how I sculpted you, and built you
How I put the stars in your eyes so you would try to reach them
I learned how humanity works, intertwined in heartstrings and sacrifice
Throwing my body into fires to forge your smiles
But when you stopped smiling at me, I knew I had done something wrong
I started wars on your behalf because I knew you would win
And for you to look up at me and smile
That would have made it all worthwhile
The thing is, the planets are slowly but surely drifting away from the sun
I created seas from my tears, so you didn't have to hide in the shade
When my effort to make you happy ended up making you uncomfortable.
The moment you cut off your wings, I grew furious
So I flooded the Earth so you could see my might
As my waves tore my own murals and statues down
My own art abandoned me, I had to understand a demon can't
When I held you in my heart, the way Venus does Cupid
You thought my ribs were a cage and broke them as you crawled
and scratched your way out
All I ever did was worship you

Reflection
by Gavin Wood

I am a reflection of past mistakes
I wonder if I will ever go unnoticed
I hear familiar sounds and I remember
I see the places I've been and I'm reminded
I want to feel the way I did in September
I am a reflection of past mistakes
I pretend to go on unbothered
I feel trapped in my own skin
I touch the walls that confine my memories
I worry that I'll never forget
I cry when I am tortured by my past
I am a reflection of past mistakes
I understand that things can't go back to normal
I say I hate you and I'm lying to myself
I dream of the moment my heart will go numb
I try to break the mirror
I hope to never see myself again
I am a reflection of past mistakes

Reality of Fear
by Meggan McLellan

What do you do when your thoughts are trying to impale you
and words want to slit your throat? Where can you hide?
I can tell you one thing, you can't hide under the blankets like a child.
This is no children's game. They will find you.
Every second you waste trying to hide, trying to outsmart them,
trying to escape, is torture.
Agonizing torture that will make you beg any god that will listen
to grant you the mercy of death.
Then you will remember; these are your words, your thoughts,
and you will try to confront them.
This will only make your pride want to set you on fire
and your cowardice want to drown you. More to be hunted by.
You will run, try to find a door.
As you see an endless hall of doors, you try every handle within reach.
All locked. You wonder if you will ever see the people you love again?
Now comes your heart, wanting to tear itself from your chest
and watch your body collapse to the ground.
You keep running, breathlessly you run into a mirror.
As it shatters you catch your own eye in the reflection of your tear-stained face.
From the shards arises your vanity, wanting to slash your wrists
and push you into a pool of sharks.
The six draw closer and closer, finally, you break.
You turn to look them all dead on.
As they engulf your being, you can finally breathe.
For the only way to be free of your issues, is to accept them.

Unnoticed
by Heidi Willy

There is an unnoticed beauty
In the bare, leafless branches of the winter worn trees.
To many, they are
death
To me, they are
Life
The leafless branches
Are long fingers reaching for the heavens
Almost as if the tree
Is trying to take root in the sky
To bring Heaven and Earth
Together.
The leafless branches
Are long spindly veins of our earth
Almost as if the tree
Is trying to carry humanity
To bring us to
Peace

Angel of Melancholia
by Jina Kim

Many gaze upon me with desolate eyes.
Few grow furious, few grow weakened to their souls.
They blame me for showing this, for they only grow with sighs.
But they never look through me, for the truth within surpasses the glass.
All faced with blindness that barricades their eyes, the celestial lies.
I despise the one who comes apparent at night, gleaming down its radiance.
Once lured, the heavenly and pale face, speaks of the wooing devil's hassle.
Pathetically blinded, they audit to the false distortions
spoken by the deceitful tongue.
Settled in one corner, I view and emulate the rosy-pink wall every day,
which has faded in tone from time.
For I stay in that one place for she comes to view herself day by day.
She dabs her colorless cheeks with softness, that of blossoms.
She utilized the dull colored lipstick onto her bare lips.
I observe her beauty, the beauty that glistens
even without the works of the white veil she applies.
Her eyes were like two fixed jewels upon her divine visage
but always seemed to be gravitating below.
For she was an angel, an angel who spoke no words through her alluring lips.
Her once-fragile bosom, became emptiness
but fragments of bitter-sweet memories scattered.
I, as a piece of glass, can do nothing but to just hang here.
Nothing but to incapably be something she may only reflect upon on.
My fair lady, once again dismayed with a dis-satisfactory expression,
once again walks away from me.

A New World
by Cristian Ciuche

In a world where materialism had doomed us
Poverty and greed's overwhelming treachery was a promised preposition
The lack of words was also something to be promised and followed
Why how else could you keep people blinded, by making them mute you see
But the silent protest within people's bones has been whimpering for much too long
Their silent screams now started screaming much louder
than those pitiful words could ever explain
So what did we do, we created
A whole nother language
A whole nother world
A whole new way
Where the dismal shadows of things which went by unspoken were now,
In an outburst of light
We wouldn't turn our backs away with the knowing of the suffering
present in front of us
The world has been sleeping for much too long
For much too many eternities of somber slumbers have passed
The oppression has come to an end
And humanity, humanity has begun once again

Summer
by Tehya Campbell

It's getting warm
Keeping up with grades, is frustrating, homework
Studying is like torture, it's stressful, exhausting,
Sitting in a class for hours, ending up doing not as well
As you thought you would on a test is disappointing,
It's getting warm in here
It's getting warm enough to wear shorts
The sun hitting my skin, no more sitting in class all day,
Listening to teachers talk
More of sitting at the lake all day, listening to waves
Campfires smoking, the wood crackling, flames dancing
Forming a circle with your friends to roast marshmallows
It's finally getting warm again
No more school, more time for friends,
more time for myself, stress free and worry free
No more studying, ruining your sleep schedule
More endless nights of staying out all night and sleeping in all day
It's warm enough to wear shorts
Warm enough to burn your cheeks and bronze your skin
No more red noses from the cold, the skies are lit up with gold
No more bland classrooms, white slushy roads, or frigid snowstorms
The humid thunderstorms, green grass, blooming flowers,
And bugs buzzing around in the air are all wonderful signs of summer,
It's finally warm

She Was Once a Happy Girl
by Briana Vargas

She was once a happy girl
Her midnight mane flowing with the wind
You'd always see her pick flowers, draw or laugh along with her friends
Everyone just simply adored her
Then there came a mean boy
He would tease her and cause her eyes to water like a waterfall
But one day, her porcelain cheek was decorated with a vibrant red handprint
Her face wet from tears, her once airbrushed smile now turns into a frown
that could even make God cry
Then she snapped
2 hours later, she's put into a place where people like her are contained
The moment she stepped foot in there, she loathed it
Later, her mother comes to visit
What she saw next, broke her aching heart
Her daughter's beautiful hair, tamed and lost its shine
Dark green scrubs now hang from her petite body
The smile on her face is now replaced with a sullen frown
Her eyes were dull and had lost all their glimmer of happiness
She wasn't dead, no, but her soul had disappeared
along with her purehearted spirit
She was once a happy little girl

After Irma
by Cody Wilson

The wind that caused it all.
It came carrying rain, it came carrying debris.
The popping of drops hitting the ground
and the snapping of branches falling from their parents.
If they weren't special to the parents, I don't know what is
but this tree was special to me, as I had part in its planting.
It wasn't destroyed, but it was toppled.
Knocked off its throne that it had retained, by the wind, and the rain.
I watched when it began, limbs being pushed to the side but standing tall.
For being as tall as a man it could hold its own against the oaks.
It was not thick, it was not connected, but it was rooted to the ground
with years of caretaking and compassion.
This time was different, the rain and the wind were pushing hard.
Harder than they had in the past, causing more limbs to fall
and it to sway more than oaks.
There was nothing I could do but watch it and be as powerless as it was
against the storm that controlled the direction of its falling.
When I found it after the storm pushed into the ground, roots up ...
I knew the wind had gone.
There was nothing I could do but push it back up and hope for it to return.
To return to the throne that it once held, amongst the yard and the forest.
The throne for a tree as tall as a man, but as mighty as an oak.

My Headache
by Tre Salyer

My headache is pain that's here to stay,
I don't think it will go away,
All I want to do is make it stop,
Because all I hear is a repeating noise in my head,
I would rather be home trying to rest my aching head,
My headache.

He Was Undersized
by Ryan Boval

He was undersized
compared to his peers
He waited for his chance
to catch the toss
He ran the final points
that clutched the win
Cheers and chants
Circulated the arena
The fans stood tall
and celebrated happily
He took it all in
smiling shyly
It was his only touchdown
of the season
He was a one-time hero
He was a hometown hero

Dark Days
by Lauren Young

Dark days, they last a little while
Dark days, put on a fake ol' smile
Dark days, you're living in one now
Dark days, they're a living hell
You're sitting on your bed, just thinking of him
Scribbling away with your trustful pen
Your hair is up, and your mind is out
The darkest days are a reality now
To the scribbles on my paper
To the lies on my face
I say that it's okay, but it'll never be the same
The way he smiles to the way he marks the mile
Has it been a while?
We have no right to fight, but do or die
Dark days are upon us
We must rush to the light

War Never Changes
by Jordan Belcher

Death and destruction of the world
War never changes
History has repeated itself time and time again
Through decades of sorrow and sadness
We never learn
We never learn

Friends
by Payton Munson

Whose friend is that? I think I know.
Its owner is quite happy though.
Full of joy like a vivid rainbow,
I watch him laugh. I cry hello.
He gives his friend a shake,
And laughs until her belly aches.
The only other sound's the break,
Of distant waves and birds awake.
The friend is slim, excellent and deep,
But he has hopes to keep,
After cake and lots of sleep.
Sweet dreams come to him cheap.
He rises from his gentle bed,
With thoughts of kittens in his head,
He eats his jam with lots of bread.
Ready for the day ahead.

One Day
by Diana Johnson

I like to dream
of amazing accomplishments and the extreme
to travel the Earth
hoping one day to find my worth
to rejuvenate my soul
experiencing the colorful cultures in whole
pushing my body to the verge
looking to the four oceans to submerge
ascending Mount Everest in all its glory
steadily calculating and pursuing my story
venturing into the profound unknown
perceiving the bountiful shapes and vibrant colors of stone
I know that one day perseverance
will be the crown of my clearance
all good things desire a wait
but I am content if this be my fate

My Love
by Dayea Greenwood

My Love, whispers sweet nothings in my ears
He never fails to open the car door
My Love makes my heart happy
He never is a bore
He makes me cry the happiest of tears,
My Love

Clockwork
by Michael C. Falanga

Time, is it a "what" or is it a "who"?
Unpredictable, unknown,
But reveals its plan as it passes,
Slowly guiding us to our destinies, our purpose.
This untouchable force though see-through, is impenetrable.
And yet its delicacy is unlike no other,
For each step taken by time affects the unseen.
Time has been experienced, will be experienced,
In what can only be described as past and future.
And over the course of this period one may never forget,
For time is not forgotten, but misplaced.
And though time's message may be unclear,
One may take comfort in the truth,
That time is there.
So I ask you again,
Time, is it a "what" or is it a "who"?

Masks
by Kaden Sterkenburg

People like to wear masks
Masks of joy and happiness
But they're not to hide pain or sorrow
What the masks hide is something sinister
They hide the rage and the hatred
They're formed by society's "moral code"
Everyone has one, encrusted on their face
Only the wearer knows what lies below
However, hard as they are, sometimes they crack
The world can see the person's true self
The crack causes destruction and despair
Other masks may be weakened, and the blight doesn't stop
But don't worry too much, they can always find a new face
So, my dear traveler of life, be wary
For behind every mask is a killer watching, waiting
Listen, because every minute, every second, there might be a new "crack"!

Stone Heart
by Tyler Untermeyer

She told me she loved me
And I knew that that was a mistake
I knew I could never hold that weight
Trying only destroyed me more
And yet I kept going and going
And now there's nothing left of me
But the realization
That your heart was stone
And all you did was break my bones

Man's Blight
by Angela Ramsey

About the long-forgotten humble man,
Above the drainage ditch he lie
After heart's longings were on ban,
At every breath, there procures a sigh.
Below the man in this black pit,
By the darkness there resist few
For which the place is used to spit
From the depths of soul torn in two.
In some unknown, ancient betrayal
Of peace and trust of all mankind,
On man's innocence is the sale,
Over which cruelty is considered kind.
To say compassion lacks a home
Only ups the price of your eternal stone.

The Wilderness Between Pages
by Cassidy Cassel

Rain pattering against the windowpane, its patterns blissful and joyful,
Outside, the lonely oak stands, its branches spread wide, catching drops carefully,
My tea steams, the aroma pleasant and kind, warmth on a cold, gloomy day.
The book in my lap speaks stories; it whispers an adventurous language,
My grey eyes soften, my toes curl in cozy socks, I'm content, clear,
My imagination runs wild behind my closed eyelids, the pages calm.
I'm running through a wood, my eyes glowing in the midnight air, clear and bright,
The scent of dirt clings to me as my bare feet tear across the blooming earth,
Laughter upon my lips, the freedom is exhilarating and savage.
I am with them, the mirth gliding about on a summer breeze, gentle, soft,
We are beasts in the darkness, unknown, carefree, like spirits of the forest,
Eyes glinting, we are predator and prey, so much more than what I dream of.
For a moment, behind my resting lids, I am one with them, those creatures,
For once, I am not caged within the gates of manners and society,
Bewitching barbaric beings of the woodland, one of the wild things.

Lost and Found
by Carson Griffin

After the war's end
For you I hunch and bend
By the shivering seaside
Below the cliffs on the wayside
In my effervescent dreams.
Over yonder I had found
On top a cliff, just standing around
To my eyes a blatant disguise
Of nature not, though releasing cries
At the windy shore, rusting beams.
Up the path did I sprint
From the sand, for I spotted a glint
Above the ocean, by the water
About some rust, I finally found my daughter.

Repressed Tears
by Mariah Thompson

I feel my best friends lately are the tearstains on my cheeks.
The person holding me on the shoulder is the daily midnight depression.
The only breath I get away from the interaction is sleeping the pain away,
as soon as I wake up I feel his welcome running through my veins
constantly reminding me of how affected I am by this virus.
His intimate kisses taking the breath from my body, leaving me for air,
when I try to resurface or call for help, he forces my voice away,
puppeteering my emotions a certain way as I smile.
Depression takes several forms
but it's the world that has taken a way to mold to it.

Drawing Blanks
by Abby Perpich

the artist stares into the canvas blank.
he ponders if there is a reason why
he cannot make a world out of the sky.
the waters harshly meet the air so dank,
the winds would whip said waters to the bank.
the people waltzing hand-in-hand, he sighs,
the whole of them would wield their white-veiled lies.
he wonders if there was a god to thank.
an artist thinks he'll never find a muse.
his town has nothing interesting in sight.
his canvas glares in such a fit of rage.
he looks around for any kind of clue.
but when he glances back to canvas white
he finds a home, his home, inside the page.

Uncertainty
by Bryce Nunn

Do I dare?
Do I care?
Do I bear to make a choice?
Do I rejoice at the feeling of uncertainty?
Do I disturb my fate?
Do I set a different date?
Do I dare ...
Do I dare ...
Do I dare to take a chance?
Do I glance at the glass of life as half full or half empty?

A Silent Voice
by Diego Garcia

The mornings and nights are the same to me
I can't tell time
I can't tell days
Because every day is a torment.
I've done bad things, I admit that.
But no one deserves to be treated like a pest, a rat
Shunned by society, I no longer long for attention
Instead I walk looking down, not looking, not listening
Deaf and blind is my perspective of society.
I suffer on my own to avoid worrying about the ones who care about me.
I try to speak about my problems but nothing comes out.
Like sleep paralysis. I talk but nothing comes out.
Because of my actions I've been cursed
Cursed by a silent voice that can't be heard.

The Debate
by Robin Fredsall

Knowledge, Wisdom and Common Sense got into a fight,
To see if the concepts of good and bad were truly black and white.
Common Sense spoke first in the heated debate, her voice above a scream,
"Wrong is wrong and right is right, there is no in-between!"
"I disagree," refuted Knowledge, and his voice got rather scary.
"We have no standard for wrong or right; they're clearly arbitrary."
The two fought for quite some time, until Wisdom chimed on in.
"Your statement has a fallacy, Knowledge," said Wisdom with a grin.
Then Wisdom turned to Common Sense and gently said to her,
"You can't play judge, jury and executioner."
"Then what is good and what is bad?" cried Knowledge and Common Sense.
"You clearly think you're right so, what's your logical defense?"
"Forgive me friends, if I am wrong. I'm not a problem sleuth;
But in order to find what's good and bad, one must first find what's truth."

Life Lessons
by Lorna Radcliff

I'm learning to stay quiet
And I'm learning to open up more
And I'm learning to breathe
Not yell when I'm frustrated
I'm learning to not be gullible
And I'm learning to not trust everyone
And I'm learning to let go
Not hold on to fantasies
And I'm learning to exercise
It's much easier to be honest with you about how I feel

People Prefer Petals
by Wardah Zafar

People prefer petals,
The partial part, the partial piece.
The particular petal is pleasant.
People perceive it as pretty and proper;
Perfect and pristine.
They care not for corollas,
The complete cut, the complete crop.
The comprehensive corolla is critical.
They consider it as crass and coarse;
Crude and criminal.
Petals are a portion,
Corollas, the whole thing.
People focus on the little bits,
Often forgetting the coming hits.

My Person
by Breanna Faulkenberry

I love my person to the moon and back,
He doesn't know that he is my whole world,
Sometimes I want to say, "Hit the road, Jack,
I cleaned up your very huge mess when you hurled."
I despise our love/hate relationship,
I wouldn't want anyone else for me,
Last date we went on we did diving flips,
Can we go climb a humongous oak tree?
I know I make no sense but I love you,
I would do anything for my one love,
I want to scream I love you till I'm blue,
At our wedding we will have tons of doves.
Please do not ever leave me all alone,
You are absolutely handsome all grown.

Green Is the Color of Nature
by Abigail Jones

I see the sun shining through,
as the birds fly away.
I feel as though, weight of rain
has been lifted off my shoulders.
I taste the fresh crisp air,
flow into my lungs
I smell the damp dirt and the green beauty
that surrounds me.
I hear the deer munching on the grass,
and the birds high in the trees calling.

Dream Or Reality
by Faith Gill

Scared and broken.
Lost and alone.
Eyes on me, wake up, they say, this is not a dream, it's reality.
Heart aching, heart racing, hands are shaking.
Breathe, calm down, just stare at the ground and don't make a sound.
One mistake and they all think I did wrong.
They all say Heaven is not for me,
That I'll R.I.P. in the pits of Hell with Satan praying at my knees.
Forced to live a lie I keep trying to deny.
They look at me with guilt, I do everything wrong in their eyes.
They don't know when it's late at night I can't help but cry.
Scared and broken.
Lost and alone.
Eyes on me, wake up, they say, this is not a dream, it's reality.

To Bear a Burden
by Charity Stephens

She carried you against her willingness,
but that won't mean she'll love you any less.
Young and beautiful, her whole life ahead.
People now stare as if her dreams are dead.
"It's her fault," yet she didn't even know
who the man at fault was who stooped so low.
In this cruel dark world, her body's your first home.
Tearing her apart, she'll have to be sewn.
To keep or discard, she'll have to decide
which choice will be best for both of your lives.
People judge either way, there is no win.
At the end of the day she lives in sin.
You may have come in a place of heartache,
but know in her eyes you are no mistake.

Sick
by Mark Mcbroom

I was sick of the lies
As I run into the night
I'm sick with myself
And now I've got no one else.
I stay at home
Lying all alone
I want to leave
But it feels as if I can't breathe
I still see her in my dreams
And now I only scream

My Dearest Roams From Sea To Sea
by Elizabeth Snell

My dearest love doth roam from sea to sea
And bears the heavy burden she is due
Though all the filth she can never accrue
I know she'll try and die to keep it free
Her face never again shall I doth see
Because she loves the sea, she loves it true
But I shall see her face in its waves too
And so I'll see her through eternity
I wish she did not have to go alone
I wish that she was not the only one
But wishes are just that, though just as stone
They will not fade away 'til they've been done
Wishes dig themselves inside your bones
And then they will not leave 'til they have won

Jamie Foster
by Ian McKinney

My dearest Jamie Foster whom I love,
Shaped are you like a beast from the depths,
You are not small and petite like a dove,
You are quite heavy, you need some more steps.
Hogging down the food like a dust buster,
My Jamie Foster, pretty she is not,
She is a liar and a trustbuster,
She is large in scale just like a dreadnought.
She is not pretty, she is pretty gross,
Her stench is like a rotting animal,
Sometimes I wish I could overdose,
Sometimes she is very tyrannical.
But for all of these things I love her so,
I love her so very very much, yo.

Spring
by Logan Smith

Eerie fog resting in existence
Yet, it is clear above
A train is heard in the distance
Chug a chug chug
But the ambient noise does not distract
From the birds and their songs
The squirrels and their chirps
And the dripping of melting snow
Through the trees the sun shines
The branches and foliage glistening
Rays of hope in these dark times

The Ocean
by Alec Barno

Below the surface, in a world of its own
There is a life of mystery of many things unknown
We'll never get to explore it all
As this place is full of limitless walls
Below the surface, the farther you go
It will be dark and pretty and make you say "whoa"
You'll see things you've never seen before
Some of them straight out of folklore
Below the surface, your eyes will drift
But you can't forget about what's above
Because the sights you see will be quite a gift
This place is ever-changing and always adapting
You don't realize it, but you are always interacting

Him
by Jordan Johnson

How can he walk around triumphantly
As I'm the one struggling to stand?
Though the aching keeps me company
Oh how this has gone unplanned.
Though my eyes deceive me
They indeed never saw this coming
I have abide the fact that like a bee
It is able to be quite numbing
As you said nothing my heart screamed
Wishing you would say more, but did not
You never said anything and now I am disesteemed
You have hit me in my blind spot
Here I stand aboding to you, and only you
It is clear to me now, that I have been cut through.

My Best Friend
by Brooklyn Ricci

I have a friend in my life,
he stands by my side no matter the strife.
I go through my days without a care,
but when I get home he is always there.
He meets me at the door with a hug,
even if I don't give him a shrug.
He goes outside to play with me,
especially when it comes to his Frisbee.
When I'm feeling down,
he always turns my frown the other way around.
If only people could be there,
like my dog the great Koda Bear.

Untitled
by Seth de Jesus

I saw her today. Carefree, reckless, full of happiness.
Well, that's what alcohol does to you.
I wanted more than ever to protect her today. She said she was fine.
Well, that's what confidence does to you.
I wanted more than ever to confess to her today. She talked about an ex.
Well, that's what expectations do to you.
I wanted more than ever to hold her today.
She came close, but not close enough.
Well, that's what longing does to you.
I wanted more than ever to kiss her today. She called a friend and talked.
Well, that's what desire does to you.
I had to leave her today. I hate that she's gone.
Well, that's what love does to you.

The Calling
by Madison Henderson

The subtle feeling like a weight pushing down on your chest,
The pounding of your heart until it feels like it's going to burst,
The sweaty palms you ball up into fists,
The moment when your feet become weights,
This is the moment God calls your name,
He whispers to your heart,
Calling you to him,
Telling you that if you come everything will be alright,
And the moment when you go,
It's just you and God,
He comforts you,
And tells you fear not my child for I am with you,
I never left you, and I never will.

Flowers In the Field
by Adreyana Brown

Flowers
Pink, Yellow
Blooming, Blossoming, Brightening
Bees Buzzing Around
Bouquet

My Love In Your Eyes
by Marcella Phelps

I stare off into the infinite hues of blue and black.
The colors are speckled with yellow, red, and purple.
The twinkling stars are near and far.
The swirling galaxies are specks in the sky.
I stare off into the infinite oceans of green.
The waters are painted in a glittering translucence.
The fish in the oceans swim along the currents in oblivion.
The majestic mermaid hides herself among the seaweed.
I stare off into the infinite universe of wonder.
The comets paint the black night with glitter.
The far-off planets look back at us in awe.
The greatest wonders are yet to behold.
I stare off into the infinite beauty.
The flecks of blue stand out against the hazel.
The pupils are wide with amazement.
The tears fall slowly with grace.

It Goes Quick
by Robert Hayer

Four years in the making, but it must come to an end
Time to say your goodbyes to every friend.
From freshman to senior, you meet many great souls
And meet many new ones when a new student enrolls.
I remember my first time walking into this school
Thinking every day would be boring and cruel.
You have many laughs, inside jokes are the best.
You make some of your own stories, leave the boring ones to the rest.
For me, it's been great, it's been really fun
I wish I could wait to say that it's done.
I remember sharpening pencils and borrowing pens,
But sadly those four years must come to an end.
I'll always remember the memories made
Just wish the end, could still be delayed.
I thank everyone for the great times on this floor
Until we meet again, it's been a fantastic four.

Brightness of Every Day
by Anela Hall

though I have not lived long
nor accomplished great things
accustomed to droughts
each day
towering over all
I pride myself transparent
nonpareil to all

Numb
by Ashley Karrim

Is it worth it,
The choices we make to feel no more?
IF the answer to this question is yes
then give me your undivided attention.
NEVER be vulnerable
avoid getting close with anyone
build walls around your heart
so big and tall, one day,
you won't even be able to find it.
DON'T hope for anything from anyone
NEVER confide in anyone and
NEVER dream of those fairy-tale happy endings.
and ... just like that we no longer are in pain
You're Welcome ...
BUT IS IT WORTH IT?

Ghost
by Nelson Marquez

You completely destroy me
You destroyed me like I never knew you could.
I'm not over you and I never will be.
The thing about love is that simple things
like her lips and her eyes break my heart.
They're not mine and I don't know whose they will be.
Her hair is the happy to my cold and bridled heart.
I used to find safety in her smile,
I used to feel warmth from the look on her face.
I've been left an empty shell to wither and fade away.
I used to think of all the things we'd be
now I think of all the things I wish we were.
I used to call you mine, but now you just don't know
what I may be left to do but stand here in the cold.
All I've got left are some photos of you and your voice stuck in my head.

Our Shoes
by Mallory Ford

Look at your shoes, do you like them?
Our shoes tell a lot about us, where we go, the type of person we are,
it might be what we do, or maybe even show our favorite color.
When you think deeply about it, not everyone has shoes.
Some people can't afford them, who are we to judge them.
Some people have them passed down, so they think of themselves as lucky
because they see that someone cares.

A Cattleman's Life
by Kyle Pridgen

My mom and dad raised me right,
They always taught me to be polite,
I don't like disrespect,
I put God first as you may expect,
That's why I respect everything,
Whether it's my cattle or friends,
For it's cattle my life depends,
I bust my butt until day's end,
To support this life I live,
I always try my best,
No matter when or where life tests,
My way of life may not be for you,
But I love it, it's true
This lifestyle isn't just for any man,
But it is for a cattleman.

Change Can Be a Bad Thing
by Brianna West

Change can be a bad thing
Especially when it comes to our grades
We try and try our best
But it wasn't enough
The high expectations turn into depression
Words start to rush into our head
Wanting us to give up
Making us think there is nothing we can do
But all we wish for is that someone would help us
Just their hand is all we need
It's a warmth that comforts us
A warmth that speaks and says
I am here for you
So please stop walking that way
I can show you the right way

Before Death Comes
by Austin Osburn

It comes for me, it comes for you.
Year in year, month in month, week in week,
Minutes to seconds, when shall it come.
Lurking in the shadows it waits,
Waiting for you, me, and all the others.
It's a predator and we're its prey.
What all may it say,
It comes every night and day.
Come and play before it fades away.
Live while it lurks around,
Soon before you are in the ground.
Hopefully you will come and stay,
Never to fade away.

What Is This Poetry?
by Kaylee Thoma

What is this unusual creativity?
This originality?
What are these clever words dancing from my pen?
What is this vision in my head again?
Is it colors and words, followed by imagination?
Or my mind simply wandering away from the station?
What is this inventive growth spurt?
A moment away from writer's block, my biggest hurt.
What is this firework of inspiration?
A talent explosion.
What is this genius moment with a relaxing-creative tone?
Could it possibly be the beginnings of a new poem?

In This World
by Alivia Kalin

Some people say that our world is corrupt, that it is broken.
But in this world, we are strong,
In this world. We build communities that can strengthen our bonds!
In this world, we, as generation 2, strive to prove what we can do as a whole.
In this world, love has no boundaries and limits to who we are.
In this world, women can raise their voices and demand their equal rights!
In this world, when we are damaged by the evil that continues to grow,
we come back stronger.
In this world, we come back ready to fight the demons that try to wipe us out.
In this world, we come together, showing the world that we are not alone,
that we won't fight alone.
They were wrong about the world, because it is healing.

Trees
by Jane Ricci

Together they might look,
But alone they must stand.
Down by the brook,
Without a helping hand.
When you lean on another
You become reliant on their support.
You make them feel smothered,
But you need the comfort.
You might be strong and tall,
But why won't you get the clue?
If they fall,
So will you.

It'll Always Be You
by Hannah Simons

It'll always be you
When times get rough
It'll always be you
When sorry isn't enough
It'll always be you
When you're sick in bed
It'll always be you
When hardships are ahead
It'll always be you
When we're now 82
It'll always be you
Forever and always, I love you

Here's To All
by Rachael Lotz

Here's to ALL
Who have had their hearts broken
By a person, by a loss, or otherwise unspoken
Here's to all who find it hard to leave bed
Because last night's dreams were just screams in your head
& here's to the people who get up to achieve
even when they barely muster the hope to believe
& here's to everyone with the past & pain behind
Because they know the future draws no one a deadline
& here's to each & everyone, whether a dreamer, student, poet
because what lies in all of you is a person
and you were never afraid to show it

Planes
by Zach Rawa

The planes are flying
As high as the eyes can see
Like a metal bird
Jets fly super fast
Jets can fly super high up
You can't even breathe
Planes are for work
But also can be for fun
Planes are very useful
Planes are expensive
Some pilots save up for years
Some say it's worth it

One Eternal Moment
by Jarrett LaCaze

We twist and turn like pieces
Of an interlocking puzzle.
Our bodies become one in a
Devilish dance as we strain
To be closer to each other.
Sweat congregates as your
Breath beats on my chest.
Every movement is precise and
Passionate with the night sky
Dancing around us, and, for
One eternal moment,
The world sang in perfect harmony.

Mountain Dew
by Nicholas Lynn

Mountain Dew tattoo
four hundred on four twenty
Look it's on my back
Seven cans a day
Caffeine keeps me up all day
Then I crash at night
Kickstart, Voltage, Ice
Live Wire, Code Red, White Out, Grape
Flavors of the Dew
Can't live without it
Mountain Dew should hire me now
Do you Do the Dew?

Autumn Changes
by Angelica Henao

My lips are dried up.
The leaves are changing colors.
The sun shied away
But clouds take its place.
A breeze of cool air swept in.
Visions of autumn
Only mean one thing.
Deer hibernated at night.
Means fresh powder rests.
It falls with no sound.
You know what season it is.
Call it out by its name.

Hopeless
by William Clarke

We use hope as a sense of strength,
we use hope to push us through our problems,
we use hope to strengthen ourselves,
we use hope in religion,
for God to help us through our struggles
and to release ourselves from punishment,
for problems we have inflicted upon ourselves.
But when all else fails,
and you blame God for not keeping you up
and not forgiving you for the wrongs you have done
That's when you know,
you are hopeless.

The Drip of a Drop
by Myshelle Kling

Drip, the sound of a single tear leaving my eyes.
Drip, the last droplet of happiness left as the others were drained out.
Drip, the pain in my head that will never leave,
only subside as a reward for submitting to the desire it gives.
Drip, the last remnant of hope I have left falls to the floor,
as I lose the last person I could count on.
Drip, the sadness falling through the slit,
leaving me, healing me, or so I hope.
Drip, the time I have left as I look at the ground thirty feet below.
Drip, the raindrop hitting the ground
I had stood before I gave in to the desire to fly.
Drip, the last drop of life as I give up.

You're the Reason
by Yanileb Figueroa

God, you're the reason why I love with such strong passion
Why I keep giving the best of me or what I have left
You already know it
You are God, everything is in your hands
But I still want to say it
Because it's what my heart feels, what it wants
Where once I felt loneliness and depression, and I couldn't go on anymore,
You came
Or rather, I let you in
You became my reason
Though I tripped many times, you still were the reason
And you'll keep being the one that all my efforts are
Because having you, doing it for you
Everything is finer, full of love
I can accept things in my life and have peace
My problems are in your hands and you always have a way to solve it
You give me so many things and you just want me to be on your side
Just to be with you and hold on, endure what comes
I thank you each day for this happiness
Because I know that even if a storm comes,
there will always be a part of Heaven in the end.

Collector
by Kamilah Wright Amézquita

I am a hoarder ... well, a collector
and it runs in the family, it kind of creates insanity.
While my grandmother collects bells, I collect seashells.
While my mother collects embarrassing stories, I collect missed opportunities.
I also collect happy, overwhelming memories and tragic, depressing memories.
My father collects gadgets and trinkets
and my little brothers collect magnets and movie tickets.
I've collected a total of ten schools
and ironically I've never once been cool.
While I collect bottled emotions,
my mother collects oceans of devotion to my dreams.
I collect friends that I've known for a little while
then it comes to an end because I can't hold a smile.
I collect beautiful jewelry that I'll never wear
and secretly I collect a truck full of misery inside my curled hair.
To be fair, I also collect madness and chaos.
I would like to share my mindset but I'd rather keep those under locks.
I collect all sorts of stuff and oddly enough I collect
the beauty and the wonder of the calm
that sits on your palms right before the storm

Quart Sized Berry Basket
by Alivia Chinsio

Purple hair smells of oatmeal
Some say she cuts it with an axe
A hen friend helping in any ordeal
Elders snort at the pea sized butterfly of lilac
That sits upon her tongue snapping wisecracks
Rumored to eat eggs of plastic
She walks carrying a quart sized berry basket
Towards the stream
The town waits her soon racket
She stands with a proud gleam
She followed the swaying balloon of steel
The town uncaring of her coming back
She did come back and it was real
Footprints left in her track
Quart sized berry basket with water sits flat
The town watched. Then following her tactic
Following in brackets
Now she was the purple haired girl living upstream
With a butterfly of placket
Rumored to eat eggs with cream

When the Wind Whispers
by Makayla Frentress

When the wind whispers
I wonder what it says
Could it speak of love, loneliness, or regret?
I often find myself precipitously swept away
By the lightest swish of breeze
Oh, I wonder what the voices of the wind would say to me
In the evenings when it hums, so light and soft
I'd like to think it's offering me solace for my thoughts
Or in the afternoons, with sharp perilous shrieks
Is that the air being stolen from me?
I might just think, probably; possibly
The flutter in the morning
Before the birds start to sing
Is that its breath serenading me?
When the wind whispers
I wonder what it says
At the end of the day, as I lay in my bed
I beg to hear something
Anything
Besides the cyclone in my head

Dark Like a Heartbeat
by Azmiveth Atkinson

It's dark like a heartbeat,
Thumping and beating.
The ribs are its cage,
But the monster is fleeing
"Don't let it escape!"
It's a twisted, starved being,
Eating everything in its path,
But we can't control feeling.
It's winged and fanged
And dripping with whispers;
It's invisible and cold
And wracked with shivers.
"You mustn't let the monster out."
They condescendingly say.
But do we really have a choice?
Did we let it get away?
"Back to your cage ..."
I beg and plead, but the monster,
Dark like a heartbeat,
Simply pays no heed.

A Wonderer Lost At Sea
by Angelica Castillo

I've drifted out to sea
With a sailboat to call my home
Even though at night I am surrounded by stars
I still feel so alone.
I sail because I am a wonderer,
I wonder what awaits for me behind the pain.
I've traveled long distances
And there is so much I hope to gain.
I also hope to lose things
Dead weight that has shackled me down
Tied me to this boat
And removed my once shiny crown.
Small and petrified
Scared of a shadow that does no harm
I've spent what feels like a lifetime
Only to dismantle the survival alarm.
I sail the tides because I am a wonderer
A wonderer lost at sea
But the question still remains,
Has anyone really even lost me?

Short On Air
by Lily Parsons

Those trees so tall,
Where goes them all?
As if, humankind does not even care,
About our very own air.
Our supply is getting scarce,
However, it is only fair.
The trees scream and rustle in the air,
They don't want to go anywhere.
They wonder why we deceive them,
Killing off our roots to our empire kingdom-
Like we kill off our troops in our pursuit of freedom
When they cry in pain, but no one can hear them.
They shade us around the world and beyond,
Without them, would there be a world we can carry on?
This world is our kingdom, our very own empire,
Why let it crumple in our hands?
That's easy- for the economy and apathetic buyers,
The government just will not do enough-
About butchering our air,
Just wait until we are short of breath everywhere.

Me, a Name
by Claire Hornibrook

Claire.
Clarity. Conviction. Curiosity.
Creativity. Concupiscent. Conviction.
Words that define, but never truly reach.
The name that binds me.
Matters of curiosity that these words describe
That I am committed to
The people in my life
A fighter, I like to think
Like the Viking origins that my name can reach
Procrastination as a weakness, a sign of my meekness
Patience for those who ask, a self obtained task
To try and defend those who cannot
The name means clarity, to which I try with sincerity
To fit the descriptions assigned to the name that I sign
Stubbornness and introversion, causing a personal distortion
Of conflicting characteristics that are truly listless.
Concern. Compassion. Commitment.
Certain. Conviction. Candor.
Claire.

Indescribable
by Maci Terry

when words fail
and my mind can't comprehend,
you are still good.
when i put you first,
when i put you last,
you love me the same.
you guide my blind heart,
hold my teetering hand,
you never let me go
i am safe inside your hands.
i fall down
i push you away
though you always stay Lord,
i'm forever in your grace.
the world shakes me
life throws me around
but the rock on which i stand
shall never move from its ground.
my sovereign redeemer,
you never let me go.

Letter To My Past
by Kenyal Turner

My heart weighs heavy,
I'm off track, I'm unsteady
I'm not depressed, I'm suppressed by society,
And the tainted image it holds.
I fight these demons day and night
I cry out, but no one hears me.
I have fought the good fight,
My time is near, please
Don't shed not a tear.
I begged, and pleaded
Just for you to love me
But like Casper, you were a ghost
I look in the mirror
Oh, what a beautiful monster you've created!
Your temptation haunts me
The kiss of death invites me,
I walk to the edge, it lures me
I've endured enough pain
Dear suicide, your wish is soon to come
Dear suicide, look at what you've done.

Goodbye
by Sky Nye

Walking along the waters of time
Two paths one sees; good and bad
A time of excitement and joy,
Runs into misery and mourning
Such confliction seems surreal
To cry or to laugh
On verge of breaking
Emotions seen jam-packed
Such news traveled fast
Feeling as if shell-shocked
Comfort is sought,
With a side of despair
What once was purity,
Now dull and death-stricken
To break down suddenly,
To receive failed comforts
Once before I mourned,
Death has left another mark
Goodbye my old friend,
Say hello to the other-side

Brutal Design
by Anastasia Ehling

I am a snowflake
Sometimes I am brutally cold
But when people look closely
I am an intricate design
My edges appear sharp
Though I am soft to the touch
I am frozen from my hatred
But I melt when someone touches me with their love
For every snowflake, there is only one and only one me
When we snowflakes gather together
We are a force that cannot be beaten
The wind tries to push us away, but it only makes us stronger
Never underestimate a single snowflake
For we are also grains of rice
Just one can tip the scale
Of victory and defeat, of balance and disparity
We are all important and we all matter
Treat us with care
And we shall show you our beauty
Every one of us is a snowflake

The Mountain
by Cheyenne Crooks

I sit in a meadow
Hidden within this mountain
I sit and listen and the whispers of the wind
I feel the mountain
As she rumbles in pain
For her forests are being destroyed
I hear the river cry
For those he cared for are now fished away
And feel the mountain rise
Puffing in defense
I lie back and close my eyes
I feel a pain across my body
A pain much worse than I imagined
I feel my body rise and fall
I feel the mountain
Shouting for help
None can hear her
For all they care
Is what they make
And never about what nature has lost

The Siege of Yorktown
(From the View of a Patriot)
by Bohdi Hollman

Tyrannical rule pierces our land
Like a dagger pierces flesh
A loss would be disastrous
Victory'll make us afresh
The enemy coats burn red hellfire
As we set up our post in York
We'll bleed and fight for our freedom and rights
May tonight the wine uncork
The bullets went whizzing, crackling in cacophony
Cannons burst with might
Danger rained upon the brave men who fought
Striking them deep with fright
The Brits enduring behind their struggling walls
As we continued to bombard
Striking forward with overbearing brawn
Their power seemingly marred
At last the foe ceased and pled
Surrendering their crown
And you know what song they played that day?
"The World Turned Upside Down"

Hakuna Matata
by Johanna Greenwood

Routines are dull, however useful in life
A set plan for the stressed, unstructured sad souls
Each morning I wake at 6:00 on the dot.
Awoken, the stress resounds in my belly
I look to my mirror and with horror I see
A flawed, frightful version of me
Hurriedly, makeup is applied, hair is brushed
I must be perfect, absolutely perfect
What shade of lipstick is most attractive?
Raw Chocolate, Hot Sand or perhaps Almond Rose?
Depends on the clothes, their color and style
A felt suede skirt seems appropriate today
With a flashy crop top reading
"I woke up like this" in sparkly pink letters
I recheck the mirror and "oh, this just won't do"
Lashes are glued on and eyebrows applied
Hair ironed flatter than societal perfection
Grabbing my bags I pass by the mirror
Ashamed that I am still not perfect, not even close
But don't worry, "High school girls have nothing to stress about."

The Relinquishment of My Agony
by Meghan Landers

It's 2015 and I'm only 13
I'm weak & I'm angry, as I fall to my knees
But then I'm told of this program by friend named Elena
She said it's fun and cool, but she'll tell me more later
I'm still in pain, I'm going insane, and it's really a shame,
as my depression extinguished my flame
I eventually join the program, scared stiff with unease
Terrified of failure and just wanna scream
But I then see a team with a whole bunch of dreams
And suddenly I'm filled with a gleam ... of happiness?
My first season completed and I feel I've succeeded
The expectations and limitations of all those doctors exceeded
Season two rolls around and I'm joining cross country
My times are decreasing and I'm happy, it's funny
Then comes season three of adored Run The Streets,
along with my countless and endless injuries
My times now give me sighs, but I keep saying I'm fine
Yet my love for these people have kept me alive
I now see this place as one I call home
As I approach season four, I'm no longer alone.

Fae Guardian
by Cheyenne Witzke

The forests are the Heir's Kingdom,
Where creatures have much freedom.
As the day begins to wane,
I stare from my windowpane.
I now walk these paths made,
With the creatures as my aid.
I watch with wonder and glee,
As the Fae children play around me.
They gather around,
With such a happy sound.
Leading me away,
As April turns to May.
The Heir stands serenely,
As he sings happily.
He smiles and takes my hand,
Leading me to a wondrous land,
Where a Queen sits in mystery,
As I gaze around at their history.
She stands with grace,
Handing me a Guardian dress of lace.

What Is School For?
by Tyler Bryson

School, what is it for?
Is it for you to sit there and pass the time while I write this rhyme?
Or to be told to sit there and that your opinion doesn't matter?
What's the matter? Is the fact of the matter too hard to digest?
I must confess it was for me too,
then I opened up my eyes to realize what was going on.
I was being moved like a pawn in a game where everyone is treated the same.
Which I think is lame! They expect us to be tame! Not to go and seek fame.
To learn things I will never use again,
then again, where did that concept come from?
It was made during industrialization where individualization was frowned upon
and men and women were just expected to follow and maintain their lawn.
Now they expect us to sit in a classroom that is running out of room!
To base our intelligence on one test and find out who is above all the rest.
Then get mad if we do bad. This era makes me nothing but sad,
but schools won't do anything about it except look at me and say,
"Too bad. Now get to class so you can pass."
Our teachers are expected to live off of low pay
and then schools wonder why hardly any of them decide to stay.
That isn't a life that's strife, so tell me again what is school for?

My Uncle and I
by Hiddaya Laryea

Smiling as wide as a duck,
My uncle and I were awestruck by the waves of the ocean,
I loved him in a fatherly way,
He loved me like a daughter he never had,
But then reality hit.
He got sick,
I wasn't there to comfort him,
For I was driven away by the motions,
I didn't have any emotions,
When I heard.
Smiling as wide as a duck near the ocean,
Tears rushed from every corner, the words grew foreign,
I loved him in a fatherly way,
For my heart broke and I couldn't find the meaning of peace,
I wouldn't let his memories perish.
But he gave me a sister and I will assist her,
In her life like he did me,
I sat near the motions of the ocean
Awestruck by the waves, I was floating but this time without him,
I won't let his memories perish, for I will cherish all of them.

Flavors of Love
by Grant Steichen

Some might say love is like a jawbreaker,
Tough and hard to get into.
Though its centre is sweet,
Some say it isn't worth it.
Many give up along the journey.
Some say love is like chocolate,
Sweet, sublime, savory.
Though it is this way for some time,
Some lose their taste.
Few maintain the attraction for it.
Some would say love is like a wine,
Elegant, divine, intoxicating.
But this love needs time to mature, to grow.
Some lose patience and lack conviction.
Many gulp it down without a second thought.
Some could suggest that love is like bread,
A crunchy exterior and soft, inviting interior.
The hard shell often pushes people away,
Some say that that love is too harsh.
Few persevere to the gentle interior.

Alone
by Evan Greenwood

I am alone and afraid
full of morbid rage
for the new age
feels like I'm in a cage
I am alone and afraid
I wish I could be free
I hope they'll leave me be
in time for me to flee
I am alone and afraid
of all the people that I hate
All I can do is wait
For the day that comes my fate

Dear Half-Brother
by Alex Motazedi

Though you do not share my Y chromosome,
Or really, anything other than a mere quarter of our genes
and presumably any corresponding traits,
I have been told we share a mother–
You and I– a mother we've both oft-disappointed.
I don't really see you, not that either of us want to have to,
I largely think it's due to have time–
An eleven year gap and not much time to spare–
Our bond, or really its weakness.
You still are my brother, halfway at least.

Titanic
by Dafne Ramirez

I thought our love was unsinkable,
Like they thought the Titanic was.
I thought nothing could tear us apart.
But you had different plans.
Feeling desperate I started to cry.
While you were just laughing,
I was broken inside,
Needing you in my arms.
I felt like I would never come back.
Our love was not able to sink, I thought.
Little did I know,
How you didn't love me anymore.

Misty Forest
by Nathan Watson

Many roads I have traveled
Inns and taverns I frequent
Searching for some news about
The Misty Forest
Yellow fields, and craggy wastes

Finally I have found the place
Over the mountains, and across the sea
Reverence fills my bones
Everything about here is tranquil
Silence, and dense fog
Treasures I do hold

Stardust
by Dawson Adrean

I trace the bright fires from which we came
I realize my own ephemerality
And though I am momentary
When I watch the dancers in the sky
I stand beside Zeus and savor great ambrosia
Whether the totality is ex nihilo or by Odin's slaying of Ymir
It is moot
For when I am in this great instance of euphoria
I have created Heaven here

Day By Day
by Rebekah Schmeusser

Take it day by day, doesn't matter what anybody says
Your heart being crushed by many emotions, just like a train wreck by the ocean
One day is going swell, but the next day it's sinking into a well
Take it day by day, grieving is okay
You make my heart beat fast, you make me think we will last
You once made me feel like enough, now you made me tough
You put me last, you make me wanna pass
Take it day by day, one day it will be okay
Thank you for putting me last, so I can put myself first

The Fearful Question
by Jace Burchell

Would you take it?
The never-ending unconditional love
a gulp of never-ending time, a crisp gulp of water
Time, not real but a myth, a mental game
The chance ... the ... chance
Would you take it?
The love anew every day
and all it takes is
a gulp of never-ending time, a crisp gulp of water
to see everyone you love be gone from life
Yet you see her eyes and the sparks ignite
Would you take it?
If laid before you on a golden dish
a crystalline goblet, a singular
gulp of never-ending time, a crisp gulp of water
she knows too much, the secret must be kept safe
the sights align, the shot ready ...
Would you take it?
A gulp of never-ending time, a crisp gulp of water

Motionless
by Reece Hunsley

High school, the daily struggle to fit in or stand out
Exhausting, so I lie here
Motionless, like a corpse
Music playing in my ears
My mind alive, but not my body
Motionless, my body rots, motionless, yet images flow through my head
Adventures, swords and sorcery, the prose I've read, clips of songs I love
The girl who would never notice me.
High school, why am I here?
I drift off, motionless. My mind an enigma, my body a statue,
Tick, tick, tick,
The endless metronome, the clock ticks away, the world melts around me.
Motionless, I'm trapped! Motionless, I'm sinking!
Motionless, darkness encroaches!
Motionless, "How was your day?" Motionless, "Hey, you okay?"
Motionless, "Don't drift away!" Motionless, light opens up.
She's in front of me, her mouth moving,
mouthing the words, but I can't hear them.
Motionless. Is this reality?

Father
by Christopher Kern

I saw him lying there, I was taken out of school for this
March 10th, 2016
I remember that day so vividly, I was in disbelief actually
Why did this happen to my father?
I remember when he was ill, sitting in his room, slowly deteriorating
I remember how I would always keep him company
I didn't care if the world ended that day
Nothing in the world was as important
In the darkest times, he was always optimistic
He had this aura about him that spawned hope, an unrelenting hope
He wouldn't let up
He would always say
"One day at a time"
I saw Anubis on that day, waiting in that room for my father
He was taken from this world, by a sinister, noxious hand
I learned the importance of life and death
I remember
March 10th, 2016
I miss my father

What's In My Head?
by Allison Bates

What's in my head
In this room that cracks and aches every day
From all the times I've failed the people I care about,
To all the mistakes I made. It starts in little sections
From one bad experience to another, it grows and becomes worse
So much as that the cracks are now so worn and so broken
That they cannot withhold anymore.
Everything floods in, everything that I've put away
And ignored and didn't want to face
Now rush in, consuming me and consuming my mind
It hurts me so much that it feels like I'm drowning in this rough sea
And I'm barely able to keep my head above the water
But I don't want to drown, I want to stay afloat.
I want to make this room my own,
I want to reminisce in happy memories with my loved ones, family and friends
Hanging them up like bright, colorful pictures
Without having this negativity looming over my shoulder,
practically haunting me every day
I want to make this room my own, I plan to.

Last Moment
by Kiara Breland

The last day of his last breath
All was quiet
His face seemed content but sad
His eyes stayed shut
As his breath was weak
I felt my tears were the only ones shed
I felt hollow, empty inside
like a piece of me was lost
My heart shattered like glass
I wanted to scream, cry for his name
I grabbed his hand, still warm but fading
I spoke to him through sobs and hiccups
I told him not to go
Pleading and pleading
He could still hear yet
Of course no response would be met
I was taken away
The last I saw of him
Taken away covered in white, cold.

The Shadow
by Shellby Galinski

The translucent shadow hides his face he has masked
is standing in a middle of a war of what he was and who he is
Scared of what his friend might think
knowing he must leave his past self behind.
The translucent shadow struggles to find his way
but he finds his way with others alike
paving his own path showing others
who he was and who he is can get along.
The translucent shadow with all eyes on him
wants to show peace, to show the world
he was once one of them but had changed
and knowing he was the only one who could end this war
as he knows what it's like on both sides of this war.
The translucent shadow takes a leap out of the dark shadow
revealing who he is, making himself vulnerable
walking down the white path
shouting let this war end, let this war end.

I See the Good
by Reagan Englett

We are all born pure, we know no evil.
We smile at pretty things, cry at scary things, laugh at funny things.
We have no self-insecurity, we can't see others' weaknesses.
Though as we continue to grow, the more we see, the more we know.
The more that we go out and do, the worse people become to you.
"Hurt people, hurt people."
Sometimes evil likes to disguise as everything we think we need in our lives.
People are gonna lie, cheat, steal and kill.
That doesn't mean everybody will.
Throughout this life we're all gonna deal with a lot,
but if you only see the bad you'll just close off your heart.
While difficult it may be,
actively choosing to see the good leads to positivity.
There is a story behind each and every scar.
A reason as to why they are how they are.
No matter how wrong they may do me,
I will keep looking for the good and good I will see.

Through My Eyes
by Madison Ingmire

Through my eyes, everything is different, everything has a certain dye
Something that sets them apart, something that makes them a work of art.
When you look through my eyes, you look for the best out of everyone
and that will never change, no matter what you do.
I'm willing to look past it- if you do, too.
Through my eyes, people are the books that need to be read,
their stories about all the tears needed to be shed.
You flip through the pages and you learn about their memories and their cages,
you look deeper than what's written on their pages.
Through my eyes, everyone gets a chance,
everyone is equal.
And it is fair.
So maybe you should start looking
Through my eyes
So you can finally understand.
So go ahead- look
Through my eyes

Untitled
by Amber Gutierrez

What is the most misused word?
Well "love" is pretty common, don't you think?
It's ironic to hear that word roll off your tongue so often.
And no sweetie, you don't have to waste your precious time saying
I haven't abused that word, like if it was a drug.
Believe me I didn't just abuse it, I was addicted to taste those very four letters.
I fooled a few. I mean, we all have.
And when we saw their heart shatter and pick up every last piece
because they finally understood the simple three words "I love you"
were just another spoken lie.
Did we ever experience that rush of adrenaline
going through our veins like we expected?
Maybe? Oh, you said no.
It was silly of us to think we'd feel victorious
because we hurt them just with one word we didn't mean.
Well, let's all take a second to remember
that words are more injurious than anything.

Dear Romeo
by Angel Dobry

I'm remembering those nights
The nights you were here
Those nights before you went there
When we would lay in the hammock and stare at the stars
The feelings we felt with the stretched and worn fabric underneath us
Your fingers running through my hair
And every word you said melted as you spoke
Sometimes they sounded like honey and sometimes they tasted like rain
When it got cold and we cuddled, almost merging into one
When we laughed so hard that we cried rainbows
I figured we would stay together for forever
But I guess I was wrong, because nothing lasts forever
That day when you gave up, I gave up too
Just not in the same way you did, I gave up on you
I've moved on now, I've changed my name, I play a different game
And though I still have these scars, I still look at those same stars.
Love, Juliet

The Idealist 5:29 a.m.
by Tiffany Rivera

the realist
sitting wistfully at a typewriter
with worn pages and letters being in places they have no business being.
they knew the thing wouldn't work
but with shortcomings in change
that would be the only option
they scan multitudes of penciled writing
they promised to type that very morning.
but an owl's hoot alerts the truth
and now slung over the table, the realist wonders why he ever tried,
spotting thick paper and a bottle of graying ink set atop his cabinet
only visible from that very same slumped position,
now his drooping lids open with a loud BANG!
then he sits upright with different materials
and attempts to do his papers like he had wanted all day.

Cord of My Heartstrings
by Gavyn Cooper

Play me a cord of melody.
Find it strong and hummed along.
Find a heat for my heart to thump along to.
When it dies down, so do I with my last note.
Tell me, can I play for you a song.
A song I wrote for myself and told to be locked in my brain's heart.
Can I play you the cords to my mind and hope you'll understand.
Please help, if I die of anxiety before I string a cord.
Call the doctor and pronounced me alive inside but dead in my head.
As the beat will still play, so will I, in my head.
The soft humming of the lady who waits at the bar to be picked up for an hour
by a sweetheart in the mood dies as the bar closes,
like my eyes from the shock of my thoughts.
Burning inside my head like a karaoke song playing on repeat with no singer.
Just the cords to play along, to find someone to hum my song.

I'm Fine
by Breanna Chitwood

I'm fine
with the names
I'm fine
with the bullies
I'm fine
I'm ignored
I'm fine
with people who leave and don't remember me
I'm fine
with having to hide my pain
I'm fine
that I take special pills that are supposed to make me feel better
I'm fine
that no one notices
I'm fine

My Beautiful Land ... Where Are You?
by Andrea Mendoza

My beautiful land ... where are you?
Between your mountains I want to get lost
Your landscape I want to see
In the city I want to be
My beautiful land ... where are you?
On the fringe of my dreams
An oasis in my soul
My beautiful land ... where are you?
In my blood your essence runs
My skin, a racial blend
A mix of cultures in the streets
My beautiful land ... where are you?
When lost, I return to that oasis in my soul
And remember where I came from
My beautiful land ... where are you?

Someone New
by Faith Stenger

I sit here in this old wooden desk
Staring out the window
My thoughts are taking over my head
Don't bother asking what's wrong, no one can know
My emotions are different every day, I cannot be read
I am trying to change
To get over this war
My power is out of range
My head hurts and my heart is sore
I don't appreciate the pain you bring me
I don't deserve all this self-hate
Being a coward is not what I want to be
It's time to open my eyes and realize it's not fate
This love we share is not true
Time for me to resign and find someone new.

Until the Storm Passes
by Cynthia Starner

Her voice shatters the very plane that we exist upon,
It rips open the sky and shakes the earth underneath us.
Her tears pelt our windows as we stay shut inside our houses.
They stream steadily down the street towards the sewer drains,
Flowing into the ditches we've carved into the earth like scars into raw flesh.
Her lights flash in the corners in our eyes,
as the smell of ozone flirts with the air.
Small children hide underneath blankets as her voice rumbles across the skies,
And frantic sirens scream out into the air, "Hide! Get to shelter!"
She slaps trees back and forth with her breath,
ripping them from the ground as her tears continue to fall.
And just as they start to wonder, if her rage will ever end,
Her tears begin to slow, and her breath is no longer labored.
At last, she reveals the sun,
And finally, the storm is over.

The Weight of the Sea
by Tyler Bro

I look ahead but cannot see
I try to swim but collapse under the pressure
I try to breathe but choke instead
I wonder what might become of me
if I fall at the hand of my oppressor
and I allow myself to be a member of the dead.

What's Wrong With Me?
by Bethany Matcham

Am I weird?
I mean I must be
Why else will nobody talk to me?
Is my face disfigured? Do I have a rash?
Do I have an extra finger? Or even an extra toe?
No, there is nothing physically wrong
Well then, why else will nobody talk to me?
Do I stutter too much? Do I whistle my S's?
Am I slow? Am I stupid?
No, there is nothing mentally wrong
Well then, why else will nobody talk to me?
What if it isn't me? What if it is you?
What if you are closed-minded? What if you are intimidated?
Yes, there is nothing wrong with me
Well then, there is something really wrong with you

Power of Love
by Isabella Iarriccio

Love is one of the most strongest things in the world
Love can put you in two moods
It can have you jumping and swirled
Or it can have you heavy in heartbreak wishing you can emboss the dude
Boom and whack
I felt like my heart went crack
I was mad and had fear
You ought to love me but that didn't stop my tear
You taught me well and I have learned from my past
You are vile and coil and definitely my last
I thought we would last still but now I know nothing lasts forever
I was aghast and I quaked, you were clever
Time heals the heart
Something came at me hard and it's gone now
I finally removed the dart from my heart

On Loving a Girl
by Lex Stewart

She is soft,
Warm to the touch.
And she is everything
You could have ever wanted.

Fire
by Haley Murray

I often feel like fire.
Burning bright and vibrant.
Happy and warm
People have fun and enjoy me around
But when times get tough,
And my flames burn out,
They pack up and leave.
The only way you could tell I was present,
Is from the cold, black ashes that surround me
No one remembers me until it's cold again
But by then it's too late
I'm too far gone and too cold to ever return
I get replaced.
Because I'm just a fire.
Here one day.
And gone the next

Good-Bye Senior Year
by Chassity Clinton

As freshmen we are terrified.
We fear what is coming our way.
We have freshmen pride.
We watch what we say.
As sophomores we try to do our best.
We still have fear.
We try our best on tests.
But we try not to shed a tear.
As juniors we are almost done.
We try to be happy.
We try to still have fun.
But we might be a little nappy.
As seniors we finally made it.
We might be sad.
We try to make senior year legit
But overall we are glad.
Comes to the point of goodbyes.
All the seniors try not to be scared.
Some of us will cry.
But all of us are prepared.

3rd Place

Katherine Wang

My Doll
by Katherine Wang

Craning my neck around those corners,
My fingers forming a fist around my soft, cloth hoodie strings.
Running through the list over and over, what's left?
The white, fluorescent lights above my head,
Burning my eyes, hotter than the sun.
Hung on my hands, baskets full to the brim
With a loaf of bread, peanut butter, jam and plastic knives.
A gaggle of gangly children pass me by,
Pushing their cart, creaking with
The weight of sweet, sugary, strawberry pastry cakes.
A distraught mother chases in despair.
"No Pop-Tarts!"
Somewhere, the distant beeping of the checkout
Pings as painful as daggers in my ears.
Making my way to the lines, the dreaded lines,
Where everyone is silently judging, a bunch of hawks.
For my purchase is just outside the norm,
A high schooler, bringing home groceries like a soccer mom.
My veins are snakes, my blood is thick and sluggishly pumping.
I just wanted a sandwich.

2nd Place

Graham Everhart

Window To Whatever
by Graham Everhart

I come home.
I bear the burdens of textbooks and text messages,
of unanswered questions and unquestioned answers.
Life was, is—always has been, always will be—messy.
No thing perfect, no place pristine, no person pleased.
Second Law of All Dynamics.
I sit down.
My textbooks and text messages are set aside,
my questions and answers will cross-pollinate on their own time.
I have work to not do. Mess to not clean.
Fade out the peripheries, tune out the surroundings,
block out the voices.
Sacred isolation.
I boot it up.
The backlight flares, the pixels twinkle,
the feel-good power chords storm the neodymium,
I browse, I fantasize. I consume, I self-delude.
Open new tabs, probe new ideas, fall down new rabbit holes;
get lost in how perfect and pristine
and pleasurable the desktop computer
and its window to whatever can be;
then get back to work.

Kimmy Daniels

Kimmy's award-winning poem was submitted
while she was a senior in high school.
Having been published by us three times,
she is now thrilled to be a Division Winner.
Kimmy is currently enrolled in Public Relations
at Kent State University,
where she continues writing
and contributing to the school's TV station.
Congratulations!

Wildfire
by Kimmy Daniels

my parents fell out of love
screaming silently
they never fought, it was only
tight lipped smiles and
white knuckles on coffee mugs
not listening when the other spoke
and finding a way to disagree
on anything that required an opinion.
the passive aggression in the air
felt so hot, like a wildfire tore through and
only burned the parts of their heart
that brought them together in the first place
and when it ended it wasn't brutal
it was just tears across my father's face as he
gathered the gumption to finally speak and say
"I'm going to be moving out"
and even when you are prepared for something to happen
you are never prepared for how it is going to make you feel

Index
of
Authors

Index of Authors

Index of Authors

Index of Authors

Index of Authors

Futures
Price List

Initial Copy 32.95

Additional Copies 25.00

Please Enclose $7 Shipping/Handling Each Order

Must specify book title and name of student author

Check or Money Order Payable to:

The America Library of Poetry
P.O. Box 978
Houlton, Maine 04730

Please Allow 4-8 Weeks For Delivery

THE AMERICA
LIBRARY OF POETRY

www.libraryofpoetry.com

Email: generalinquiries@libraryofpoetry.com